C
A
L
L
E
D

CALLED

Jonny Gumbel

Foreword by Archie Coates

God's purpose for your life and how it
changes absolutely everything

Muddy
Pearl

Published in 2024 by
Muddy Pearl, Edinburgh, Scotland.

www.muddypearl.com

books@muddypearl.com

British Library Cataloguing in Publication Data.

A catalogue record for this book is available from the British Library

ISBN 978-1-914553-27-1

Typeset in Minion by Revo Creative Ltd, Lancaster

Printed in Great Britain by Bell & Bain Ltd, Glasgow

Teach me to do your will,
for you are my God;
may your good Spirit
lead me on level ground.

PSALM 143:10

FOREWORD

In the years I've been a pastor, I have found calling to be the topic people want to explore and talk about almost more than any other. Whoever we are, and whatever stage of life we're in, we find there are so many questions, puzzles and potential pitfalls to do with our calling. What am I meant to be doing? How do I know? What if I can't hear God telling me what to do? How can I be sure I'm not missing something? If I'm in my calling, why is it so painful and difficult at times? I thought I knew my calling, so why is it not slotting into place by now?

And conversations around calling are more complex and necessary today than ever. Complex because of the many options and choices available, and because we inhabit a rapidly changing world which can make us less certain and sure-footed. Necessary because our world is crying out for people who will live with selfless purpose and conviction, capable of carrying God's goodness and transformation to the people around us.

God has a purpose for every human being, and this purpose is discoverable. Nothing is more important than for us to discern and do it. The apostle Paul indicates this expectation when he writes, 'For we are his workmanship, created in Christ Jesus for good works, which God prepared beforehand, that we should walk in them' (Ephesians 2:10, ESV). Or, more punchily, 'do not be foolish, but understand what the will of the Lord is' (Ephesians 5:17, ESV).

Jonny is great at helping people figure out their calling, and grapple with all the questions and emotions that come with it. His advice is never directive or restrictive: he simply comes alongside as a companion, always curious, gently probing, reassuring and encouraging. I myself have been on the receiving end of his counsel and wisdom, and my conversations with him have led me into greater clarity and courage in my own calling, sometimes leading me to major moves, other times minor tweaks.

In *Called*, Jonny gives us the principles and guidance we desperately need in order to make some of the most important decisions in our lives. He shows us how to approach our calling through the illustrative stories of biblical characters, as well as his own experience. He conveys calling as important yet not intense. Ultimately, because we are rooted in God's love for us (the topic of Jonny's previous book), calling is an adventure to explore without pressure or fear of getting it wrong.

Discovering how I am called by God – 'according to his purpose' (Romans 8:28) – has been the most joyous and freeing experience of my life. My prayer for all who read this book is that, as well as each knowing our own personal calling, we will better help others discover and sustain theirs, and together we will be better equipped to serve the purposes of God in our lifetime.

ARCHIE COATES
VICAR, HOLY TRINITY BROMPTON

London, May 2024.

ACKNOWLEDGEMENTS

I am hugely grateful for all those who helped me to discern God's call at various points in my life, and who thereby helped, directly or indirectly, to write this book, especially my kind and encouraging parents and my brilliant and inspiring siblings.

Thank you to all those who were part of the process of discerning our call to Rio de Janeiro and who helped us to get here: the community at St Peter's Brighton who sent us, the community at Christ Church Rio who have welcomed us, Alex Cacouris who had the idea of us in Rio before anyone else, Nalishuwa Ikachana for her crucial prophetic word for us, Archie and Sam Coates and everyone in the HTB network for encouraging and supporting us, Paul and Lucy Lennard at iNET and Richard Bromley at ICS for training us, praying for us and guiding us as we set out to Brazil.

Thank you also to all those who helped with the formation of this book. I am grateful for Archie allowing me to preach lots of sermons on calling and purpose at St Peter's and writing a foreword, and for Russell Winfield for inviting me to teach on the biblical stories of calling in the 'Peter Stream' course at St Mellitus. To Stephanie Heald for encouraging me that this could be a book and for her wisdom in shaping the content, and Jez and Kirsty Wong for supplying a beautiful and peaceful space in Rio to work, as well as the staff at Cirandaia, my favourite café in Rio, for providing me with 'chocolate quente' and 'pão de queijo' while I worked on these chapters at a table in the corner. Thank you to Hannah Milne for reading an early draft and using her excellent English skills to help improve mine, and for others who read drafts and encouraged me along the way: Sam Stephens, Martha Bryant, Phil Gladwin, Russell Winfield and Nicky Gumbel.

A special thank you to Jackie Pullinger who has inspired so many of us for so many years, and who, with everyone at St Stephen's welcomed us as a family in Hong Kong for three months in 2020, taught us and prepared us for our next adventure.

And, of course, to Tara, for listening to Jesus and trusting in him when she sensed that God was calling her to marry me, to move to Brighton and then to Brazil. And for eventually reading my first book. And our delightful children, who also listened to Jesus and helped us work out what God was asking us to do.

CONTENTS

LOVED
AND CALLED

Romans 1:1–7

To all in Rome who are loved by God and called to be his holy people.

ROMANS 1:7

I believe every one of us is born with a purpose. No matter who you are, what you do, or how far you think you have to go, you have been tapped by a force greater than yourself to step into your God-given calling. This goes far beyond what you do to earn your living. I'm talking about a supreme moment of destiny, the reason you are here on earth.

OPRAH WINFREY*

You were made for a purpose. Your life is not an accident. It is not meaningless. We feel these things instinctively, and yet it's not always easy to see what that purpose might be. Life can often feel meaningless. We can feel directionless. And we can find ourselves asking what our purpose might be: what should I do and who am I supposed to be?

Deep within, we need to know that we are loved. It is also essential to know that we have a purpose. The message of Christianity is that

---

* Oprah Winfrey, *The Path Made Clear: Discovering Your Life's Direction and Purpose* (Bluebird, 2019).

there is a God who loves you unconditionally and eternally. This love changes everything. And because God loves you, he also calls you. He gives your life purpose. When you become a Christian, you become one who is both loved by God and one who is called by God. God calls us because he loves us.

In the opening verses of Paul's letter to the Romans, Paul refers to 'calling' three times. First, he himself is 'called to be *an apostle*' (1:1). There is a specific role for which he has been called: to go out to the world to preach the gospel and plant churches. Next, the Christians in Rome 'are called to *belong to Jesus Christ*' (1:6), that is, to be in relationship with Jesus, to know him and love him. Finally, they are 'called *to be his holy people*' (1:7), which means becoming like Jesus, and therefore becoming the people whom God made us to be. Here in these few verses, we have a glimpse of what our purpose will be: to do what God asks us to do, to be the people he is forming us to be, and to love Jesus and those around us.

We also find here the balance between our general calling and our specific calling. We are all called to belong to Jesus. We are all called to be holy. Elsewhere Paul writes that we are called to be free, called to hope and called to live in peace. There are many things which all of us are called to do, like being kind and compassionate, sharing what we have with those in need and making disciples of all nations. But God also has a specific calling for each of us, things which only we can do. For Paul it was to be an apostle, for Mary it was to bear the Son of God and for Peter it was to be a 'fisher of human people'.*

Previously I have written about the love of God; this book is about the call of God. This is for anyone trying to work out what they should be doing with their lives, who is looking for purpose, who is asking themselves what God wants them to do and who he wants them to be. We will look at the stories in the Bible in which

---

* Galatians 5:13; Ephesians 1:18; 1 Corinthians 7:15; Luke 5:10.

God calls individuals for a specific purpose, trying to see in them what God might be saying to each of us about our own purpose. Some of these stories are dramatic and clear; others are more subtle and confusing. Some characters have a high profile; others are more hidden away. There is no set formula for this, as God seems to adopt a different method with each person he calls in the Bible, and he continues to find new ways to call us.

This book emerged from studying these stories of calling, as well as my own experience of hearing God's voice and sensing his call at different points of my life: to Oxford for university aged eighteen, to ordination in the Church of England in my twenties, to marriage to Tara in 2009, to St Peter's Brighton for thirteen years and then more recently to Rio de Janeiro. And over the years I have loved trying to help people work out their own calling, whether it has been around jobs and location, marriage and singleness, or ordination and ministry.

Working out our calling is like swimming in the sea: most of the time we need to keep our heads down and keep going with whatever we are doing, but every now and then it's helpful to lift our heads and look around, to make sure we are going in the right direction or to ensure we're not about to collide with a ferry. This book is designed to help you to do exactly that, to lift your head and look around you, and make sure that you are living out your calling.

I encourage you to read the biblical story before you read each chapter, asking God to speak to you and guide you as you do so. My prayer is that through these stories God might speak to you about the direction of your life, and that you might hear his voice, follow his guidance and fulfil his purpose for your life.

PART ONE

Beginnings

Chapter 1

WATER-WALKING AND WHITE BENCHES

Peter
Matthew 14:22–36

Shortly before dawn Jesus went out to them, walking on the lake. When the disciples saw him walking on the lake, they were terrified. 'It's a ghost,' they said, and cried out in fear.

But Jesus immediately said to them: 'Take courage. It is I. Don't be afraid.'

'Lord, if it's you,' Peter replied, 'tell me to come to you on the water.'

'Come,' he said.

MATTHEW 14:25–29

The days of idle pleasure were over; those to come would be of harsh and enduring sacrifice. He would be confronted with unknown tasks and unforeseeable dangers, but he would be resolute and firm, clear-minded and calm, with the light of faith burning in his heart.

MACHADO DE ASSIS*

'Lord, if this is you, tell me to come.'

After twelve years in Brighton, Tara and I began to sense that God might be calling us to something new. But I wanted God to be

---

* Machado de Assis, *Yaya Garcia*, UNESCO collection of representative works: Brazilian series, tr. RL Scott-Buccleuch (Peter Owen Publishers, 1976), pp56–57.

clear. During that time, I read this story in Matthew's Gospel, where Jesus walks on water, and was struck by the words of Peter to Jesus. So I started to pray, 'Lord, if this is you, tell me to come.'

Becoming a Christian means opening ourselves up to God's voice directing our lives. Tara and I believe that God calls people, and we had felt called to Brighton all those years ago. It had felt so clear to us. On 3 January 2009, Tara and I had walked through the streets of Brighton, down from the station, through North Laine and out into Valley Gardens. We had looked up and seen St Peter's Church. Our hearts had leapt, and we felt sure that this was where God meant us to be. I proposed later that afternoon, and (eventually) Tara said, 'Yes'.

We got married that summer, moved down to Brighton, and started out on what was to us a great adventure. The church grew, as did our family. We had four children, settled into a home, made friends, and we loved the people we worked with. We imagined that we might stay there forever.

The story of Jesus walking on water begins with the words, 'Jesus *made* the disciples get into the boat and go on ahead of him to the other side' (14:22). It suggests that the disciples didn't want to do this, that perhaps they were happy where they were. I can understand this. They had just witnessed an amazing miracle involving the multiplication of food. If I were them, I'd want to stay there and see this miracle done every mealtime, hopefully branching out from bread and fish, to cake and chocolate. And they had lots of leftovers. I love leftovers. My favourite meal of the week is when we get to cook up all the leftovers. But after a long day, when maybe they wanted to stay where they were, Jesus made them get into the boat and go somewhere new.

To be a Christian is to be loved by Jesus Christ, saved by Jesus Christ and transformed by Jesus Christ. But it also means being sent by Jesus Christ. It means that he is Lord, and so he is in charge, and often he asks us to do things that we would not normally think to do or want to do. Looking at the stories of calling in the Bible, it is hard to think of many occasions when God calls someone, asking them to do something, or go somewhere, and they reply, 'Great! Thank you. That's exactly what I wanted to do. I was hoping you would ask me. When can I start?' But more of that later.

So, we were settled and happy in Brighton, and then suddenly something began to stir. It started with a three-month sabbatical spent with St Stephen's Society (Jackie Pullinger's organization in Hong Kong) in 2020. When we returned home, I had a strong sense that we shouldn't be in Brighton. This was odd because I love home. My favourite part of any holiday is coming home.

It was also in the middle of the COVID-19 pandemic. We had arrived back in England during the first lockdown, with life around us changing in so many ways. And in the middle of this global crisis, when life was particularly difficult and unstable, we felt that God was calling us to something new.

Jesus calls out to Peter during a storm, in which the disciples are being beaten and battered by the waves. We can often feel beaten and battered by the waves of life: waves of injustice, waves of grief, waves of exhaustion, waves of violence. The disciples are exhausted, for they had set out in the evening and it was now between 3am and 6am. It was dark, so they couldn't see where they were going. They were isolated and alone. And they were far from land, so the solid ground of stability, certainty and safety was not in sight.

In other words, this was not a good time for anyone to get out of the boat. If I were attempting to walk on water for the first time, I would have chosen a bright, sunny day, with calm conditions and perfect visibility after having had a good night's sleep. In the storms of life, when everything seems to be falling apart around us, we can either retreat into ourselves, holding on to what we have more tightly, simply trying to get through it, or we can open ourselves to what God might be wanting to say to us in the middle of the storm.

During that year after we returned from Hong Kong, it felt like I was being hit by wave after wave. It was not just wave after wave of COVID, but also waves of shame, waves of confusion, waves of disappointment, waves of exhaustion. I remembered reading about a surfer describing the fear of a 'two-wave hold down', which is when you are wiped out by a wave and cannot get to the surface before another wave hits you. That's certainly how it felt at some points that year.

But during that year of pandemic, when we were exhausted, beaten and battered by the waves of life, and the future was so unclear, Tara and I began to feel like God might be calling us to something new. But we weren't quite sure what. A community house in the English countryside? An island in the Caribbean? Hong Kong? New York? A theological school? It's always difficult to distinguish between the voice of God and our own natural desires.

Before Jesus calls Peter out of the boat he says to him, 'Take courage! It is I. Don't be afraid' (14:27). The call to step out will emerge from Jesus' revelation of himself, not a revelation about Peter. He doesn't say to him, 'Peter, you can do it.' He doesn't come to show the disciples their potential, but his own power and authority.

Over that year of turmoil, I wasn't sure what it was that God was calling us to, but certain convictions were becoming stronger and clearer within me: that I am a great sinner and Christ is a great saviour, and that Jesus is worth everything.

Then, exactly a year after coming back to England, a year of trying to listen and think and work it all out, I had a thought. It felt so tiny and gentle. It was nothing like certainty, nor even a conviction. It felt more like a suggestion. Tara and I went out for dinner and I said to her, 'I think we should consider Brazil.'

Tara had felt called to Brazil when she was a teenager, and in the subsequent years she had felt sure that she would spend some portion of her life there. However, it had never quite happened. She had tried a short-term mission trip there while we were dating, but she did not particularly enjoy the experience, and returned questioning what that sense of calling had been about. Shortly after that, I proposed and we moved to Brighton, and for Tara that idea of Brazil began to fade.

Twelve years on, we talked about Brazil again, and something began to stir. We remembered an email we had received three years earlier from someone called Alex about a church in Rio. I had met him once, eighteen months before this message, at the back of church at St Peter's where we had had a brief conversation about Brazil, but I had thought nothing more of it. However, a year and a half later he had been praying in the English-speaking church in Rio, asking God about its future, and Tara and I had kept coming to mind. So he sent me a message which we had quickly dismissed.

Now three years on from the email, and four and a half years since Alex and I had met at the back of church, we read the message again and wondered whether there might be something in it. I managed to get in contact with Alex (he had moved back to Dorking in the south of England) and arranged to speak to him on Zoom.

On the morning of that first conversation, I read this passage in Matthew's Gospel, and these words of Peter became my prayer: 'Lord, if it's you, ask us to come.' We spoke to Alex and as he described the church and the city around it our spirits began to rise. And it began to sound possible. There was now a vacancy at the church. There would be schooling for our children. The congregation was a mixture of rich and poor, internationals and Brazilians. It sounded intriguing. Tara and I finished the call, looked at one another, and one of us (I forget which) asked, 'What do you think?' and the other replied, 'I think we're going to Rio.'

We felt excited all that day, and I continued to pray, 'Lord, if it's you, ask us to come.' As we went to bed that night, we read the verse of the day in our Bible reading app, as we did each night. This night it was this: 'Kneel and pray ... get yourself ready; I'm sending you.'*

We began to work out if this really was for us. There were lots of complications and obstacles. There was pressure to take other roles at other churches. There would be many voices in the months which followed which caused us to question this sense of calling. And I kept praying, 'Lord, if it's you, ask me to come. Lord, if Brazil is your

---

* Acts 7:33–34, MSG, Nicky and Pippa Gumbel, *The Bible with Nicky and Pippa Gumbel*, Day 163, bible.alpha.org (accessed 23 April 2024).

will, then ask us to come. Lord, if Christ Church is your will, ask us to come.'

These things are never totally clear. Peter starts by saying, '*If* it's you.' He's not sure. The call of God is always a step of faith and therefore there's never certainty. But God in his grace often seems to give clearer signs the bigger the move we need to make. And we felt like we would need something big and clear to uproot our family and go to the other side of the world. Neither of us are naturally good at learning languages (I have enough trouble with English), and it didn't seem like an obvious fit for our skills and experience. But then, as a fisherman, Peter's skills and experience were more suited to being inside the boat, rather than outside the boat on the water, so we needed to be open to whatever God might ask us to do.

Eventually we decided to include our children in the process. We took them out for pizza, told them what we were thinking, and said that we would all need to ask Jesus what was right and listen to his voice. At that point our eldest son said that he had a picture in his mind. He said that he saw a white bench between two palm trees. 'OK,' we thought, 'there might be palm trees in Rio, and quite possibly some white benches too.'

'And there's something else,' he added. 'I see a word in white on a black background. It says, "Come."' It was the same word that Jesus had said to his disciples. My son didn't know that I had been praying, 'Lord, if it's you, ask us to come.' He just saw the word in his head and told us, and it felt like a clear indication we should pursue this opportunity.

By February the next year we were on the plane to Rio to see whether this really was what God was calling us to do. There were lots of challenges just getting there. The same child who had had the picture of the white bench and the word 'come' was in hospital eight times in the few weeks leading up to getting on the plane. Some members of the family got COVID and had only just recovered in time for the flight. When we went to the airport, we were not sure whether we would be allowed on the plane.

Then things got worse once we got there. I arrived with one of the worst migraines I've ever had. We were staying with a family in Rio, who had been incredibly kind, opening their home to a family of six whom they had never met before. But within the first four days of our visit both their cars had broken down, they lost their water supply and ran out of gas. And it was the hottest time of the year.

In my experience, once you obey God's call, life becomes a mixture of miracles and struggles. One moment it feels like you're walking on water. The next moment it feels like you're drowning. Your lack of faith is revealed, along with all your other weaknesses. Obeying the call of Jesus doesn't hide our weaknesses; it exposes them. Peter says to Jesus, 'If it's you, tell me to come to you *on the water.*' We respond to the call of Jesus, not walking on solid ground, but on the water which feels uncertain and unstable.

There were real challenges both before and after our trip. In many ways the year before arriving and the year after arriving have been the toughest I've ever had to face. And yet there were also miracles. On that trip I had hoped that we would get off the plane, our children walking hand in hand telling us how much they loved Rio, our hearts full to bursting with the joy of being in Brazil. But it wasn't like that at all. It was a tough couple of weeks. And yet God was speaking to us in the middle of chaos and difficulty.

There were three significant moments that seemed to confirm God's call to us in those two weeks. A few days after arriving we went to visit the old Anglican building of Christ Church. It was a hot and hectic visit – the building looked quite formal, and the situation was complicated by the fact that the church shared the site with The British School in Rio and some other organizations. We felt overwhelmed by the task. I slipped out the side of the building into the gardens which surrounded it, and there I saw a white bench. And palm trees. I called to my son to have a look at the bench, and he said casually, 'Yes, that's the one I saw.' It was the same design, the same shape, the same colour he had seen in his mind in a pizza restaurant in Brighton Marina several months earlier. And it was surrounded by palm trees (as well as a mango tree, and a bin).

The second moment was on the following day when we went up to visit a Christian community house in Providência, the oldest 'favela' in Brazil. We walked up the steep steps, over rubbish and excrement, past the cockerels being trained to fight, and our hearts began to stir. We spent a few hours in the house and there were moments there, seeing Tara surrounded by the children from the 'favela', that I caught a glimpse of what God had made her to do and had placed within her heart as a teenager, and I became convinced that I needed to find a way to get Tara to Brazil.

And then the third confirmation came on the last day of our trip. We had decided to take a cable car up to the top of the famous Sugar Loaf Mountain, but when the day arrived the mountain was covered in a thick cloud. Initially we decided to cancel our plans, reasoning that it was not worth the money to go up if we could not see anything. However, in the end we couldn't work out what else to do and thought a cable-car ride might be exciting for the children even if we could only see the inside of a cloud. So up we went, entering the cloud and, as we had anticipated, not being able to see anything other than the cloud. But then suddenly the cable car emerged out of the top of the cloud and we had a beautiful view of Rio through gaps in the cloud below us. And we could see the statue of Christ the Redeemer across the water, with Jesus holding out his arms to us. It felt like a picture of what we were about to do: heading into the cloud of the unknown, stepping out, not being able to see what we were doing or where we were heading, but knowing that Jesus was there already, with his arms out waiting for us.

The call on our lives is a call to Jesus. When Peter gets out of the boat he starts walking towards Jesus. He's not walking towards his destiny, heading out on an adventure or pursuing his purpose. He's walking towards Jesus. This is what we were beginning to learn. Jesus calls us and gives us purpose, but even more than this, Jesus is our calling. He is our purpose.

Chapter 2

DOING, BEING AND LOVING

Adam and Eve
Genesis 1:26–31

So God created mankind in his own image,
in the image of God he created them;
male and female he created them.
God blessed them and said to them, 'Be fruitful and increase in
number; fill the earth and subdue it. Rule over the fish in the sea
and the birds in the sky and over every living creature that moves
on the ground.'

GENESIS 1:27–28

Tony Stark: Thank you for saving me.
Yinsen: Don't waste it ... don't waste your life, Stark.

IRON MAN*

Our search for purpose can be summed up in three questions which, whether we are conscious of it or not, we are all asking: What should I do? Who am I supposed to be? And whom should I love?

We want to know what to do. Whether in the big decisions around careers and work, or in little decisions about how to spend our free time, we are confronted with the question of what we should be doing.

---

* Jon Favreau, *Iron Man* (Marvel Studios, 2008).

And the more choice there is around us, the harder it can be to make these decisions. We are also trying to work out who we are, to get to grips with our identity, to sort through our emotions and desires and personality to understand who we are meant to be. Then there are the questions about the relationships we form: getting married or remaining single, having children, making friends, the people we try to help or support, the communities where we live, and we find ourselves asking ourselves whom we are supposed to love?

We ask these questions because of the way we were created at the very beginning. For at the start of the Bible we read the story of God creating human beings 'in the image of God.' God makes the whole of creation, and then he creates human beings in his image. We are all made in God's image and therefore we are made for a purpose, and in the description of God's creation we see the answer to these three fundamental questions.

DOING

When God created human beings, it was to *do* various things, and so our purpose is to do the things which God gives us to do. So, one element of being created 'in the image of God' is *functional*. It is about the role we are supposed to have. Our calling involves *doing* things.

When God created human beings in his image it was to rule over the fish in the sea and the animals on the land, to name the animals and to participate in God's work in creation. In other parts of the ancient world, the great kings were thought to be 'the image of God', which meant that they were supposed to represent God in the world, doing God's work, ensuring there was justice and peace, and the care of the natural world. But here in Genesis is the radical affirmation that all of us have a purpose. All of us have a role. There are tasks for all of us to do. Jesus would later come to his disciples after his resurrection, saying, 'Go and make disciples of all nations, baptizing them in the name of the Father, and of the Son and of the Holy Spirit, and teaching them to obey everything I have commanded you.'* It is a call to do things: to go, make disciples, teach and baptize. Paul writes to the Ephesians, 'For we are God's handiwork, created in Christ Jesus to do good works, which God prepared in advance for us to do.'** God has prepared tasks for us to do, which only we can do.

Our purpose is *commanded*. God speaks to the first humans and tells them what they are supposed to do. They do not choose it, nor do they work it out for themselves. We are not free to decide our purpose for ourselves. A life of purpose is one of obedience to the call of God who loves us. Therefore, the call of God will almost always start with someone hearing the voice of God and responding to it.

Our purpose is *external* to us. God creates the first human beings for the sake of the world around them. They are not created just for themselves but for others. Therefore, our purpose is not simply self-fulfilment, self-realization or self-satisfaction. Our purpose is service. It is directed to the world around us. When God calls people in the Bible, it often involves him persuading those individuals to stop thinking only about themselves and to direct their attention to the people, the problems and the world around them.

Our purpose is *expansive*. God says, 'Be fruitful and increase in number; fill the earth and subdue it' (1:28). When God calls us, it is not normally to hide away or retreat. When God calls us, he calls us to go out, to go beyond the places we are used to being in and the people we are used to dealing with. This instinct within human beings can be misdirected or distorted, particularly when it takes the form of colonialism or empire-building. However, God's call remains expansive, as he sends us out to serve him in the world, and to bring his light and grace and salvation to more and more places.

Our purpose involves taking *responsibility*. God commands the first humans to 'rule', which means that we are the ones who are responsible. The language of ruling might feel uncomfortable for

* Matthew 28:19–20.
** Ephesians 2:10.

some (and perhaps very comfortable for others!), but either way it means that we are responsible. Rulers are those who (should) take responsibility. In the stories which follow we will see God calling people to take responsibility for groups or problems which they had previously not thought were their problems to worry about. Moses had decided that the enslaved Hebrews were no longer his problem. Esther didn't believe it was her responsibility to protect the Jews living in Persia. Jonah certainly did not think that the fate of the inhabitants of Nineveh was his responsibility. But in each case, God persuades them to take responsibility. So often our purpose emerges as God persuades us that something we had previously thought had nothing to do with us (street homelessness, modern slavery, inequality, English-speaking churches in Rio de Janeiro) might be our responsibility.

Our purpose is *collaborative*. God calls Adam and Eve together. He gives them a joint calling, as male and female, to operate in partnership. Calling is always both individual, for God has something specific for each of us, and communal, for God calls us together, to work together and to fulfil our purpose together. And when men and woman work together it is particularly powerful. One important element of our sense of calling to Rio de Janeiro was Tara and me sensing a calling to work together in a new way.

Our purpose is *significant*. God's call on our lives is to something important. That human beings are made in the image of God means that it is not just the Pharaoh of Egypt or the kings of Assyria who have a significant role in the history of the world. We are all made in the image of God and so all of us have a significant purpose. And so, one of the great dangers we face is wasting our lives.

When Facebook first emerged, I initially resisted it, but finally joined long after everyone I knew. However, I quickly realized that it could become a huge waste of time. Once, I found myself on Facebook watching a video of a man putting on a pair of jeans without his hands, using only a series of lunges. It was undoubtedly impressive, and fascinating on some levels, but four and a half minutes later, I realized that there may have been better ways to spend my life. So, I deleted the app from my phone and tried never to use Facebook again.

The devil will often tempt us to do things that are wrong: to lie, to gossip, to be unfaithful or unkind. But if the Enemy cannot get us to do the wrong things, he will try to get us to spend our time consumed with the insignificant things. This does not mean significant in terms of being outwardly impressive, for many of the most significant things we do may well be invisible to most people. William Carey, a cobbler from London who became a great missionary in India, wrote, 'I'm not afraid of failure. I'm afraid of succeeding at things that don't matter.'

BEING

The first part of our calling is to do the things which God calls us to do. But more important than what we do is who we are. Not only are we to do what God calls us to do, we are also to become the people whom God calls us to be. Being made in the image of God is not just functional, it is also *ontological*. It is about who we are. Human beings were made in the image of God, which means that we are supposed to reflect the nature and character of God through who we are. And so our character is our calling. Jesus would later say to his disciples, 'You *are* the salt of the earth … You *are* the light of the world.'* He would command them, '*Be* perfect, therefore, as your heavenly Father is perfect.'** Paul would write to the community in Rome, 'To all in Rome who are loved by God and called *to be* his holy people.'*** Our calling is about who we are more than what we do.

* Matthew 5:13–14.
** Matthew 5:48.
*** Romans 1:7.

In the spring of 2020, as we travelled to Hong Kong to spend some time with St Stephen's Society, I was sure it was going to be hard work. I had spent a couple of life-changing months there in my late teens, loving it, but also finding it exhausting. The day after we arrived, we sat down with some of the leaders and asked what we could do to help. They replied, 'Just be here as a family.' We thought it kind of them to give us time to settle in and get used to life there before we got to work, so we made the most of living amongst the 'brothers' there, sharing meals, welcoming them into our home, playing board games, joining in with times of worship and prayer. After a few weeks of this we asked again, 'Now that we've settled a bit more, what do you want us to do to help?' But the answer was the same, 'Just be here.'

Over those months, we did not do a lot which was obviously helpful. I did not do any of those things which I was used to doing as a pastor in England, like preaching or leading meetings. Instead, we learnt that we were valuable for who we were, just by being part of that community with very few responsibilities, simply being those who pointed people to God by who we were.

Our calling is to be the people we were made to be. But this is not always straightforward. We often struggle with our identity, feeling like we are not quite the selves we wished we were. We long for authenticity.

This search for identity is the subject of many of the great Disney films, from *The Lion King* to *Moana*. Simba loses his purpose because he forgets who he is. And so his father confronts him: 'You have forgotten who you are.'* Moana gives up on her quest to save the world, until her grandmother (in the form of a stingray) asks her, 'Do you know who you are?'** Moana only rediscovers her calling when she remembers who she is. These films remind us that our purpose and identity are inseparable.

* Roger Allers and Rob Minkoff, *The Lion King* (Walt Disney Pictures, 1994).
** Ron Clements et al., *Moana* (Walt Disney Studios Motion Pictures, 2016).

We can try to form our identities based on those around us, building them on the opinions of others, the affirmation and approval of those around us. Alternatively, we can try to form our identities based on what is inside us, on our feelings and desires. Each of these approaches can help us in some way, giving us some ideas of who we are, but neither can give us what we are looking for. Other people cannot understand us perfectly. And we ourselves can become confused by the feelings and desires which are often in conflict within us. Ultimately our identities are found in God. We were made 'in the image of God' and therefore it is in relationship with God that we discover who we really are. Self-awareness is important. Community is essential. But more than looking within or looking around, we discover who we are by looking up.

Therefore our calling is to align ourselves with God's design for us. Our purpose is to be the people whom God made us to be. For we are made in the image of God. Our identity is not self-determined. We are not our own creators. We don't get to decide who we are. Our identity is a gift from God, found in relationship with him. The same voice that directs our actions also reveals who we are.

This is important, particularly in times of frustration when we are unable to do all we wished we could do, or at times of disappointment when our actions have not led to the results we wanted. For in these times, when we might feel like we are not fulfilling our purpose, God is working on our character, which is our purpose.

LOVING

We are called to do and to be. But even more important than these is the call to love. I know this to be true in my experience with parenting. There are all kinds of things I want my children to do: to brush their teeth, go to bed on time, eat vegetables and speak and act kindly. But more important than what I want them to do is the people they are becoming. I want them to be kind and compassionate, wise and perceptive, courageous and joyful. And then even more important than their characters are their relationships. I long for them to have good relationships with each other, with their parents and friends and in the future happy marriages and happy families. More than anything I want them to love Jesus and to know his love for them. For the quality of our relationships is more important than the content of our characters.

The image of God is functional and ontological, but it is also *relational*. When God created the first humans in his image, he was making them with the ability to love and be loved, to be those who were compatible with his love. When we read of God breathing life into Adam (Genesis 2:7), it reminds us of a kiss. He blesses them, he speaks to them, and he seemingly walks with them in the cool of the evening (Genesis 1:28; 2:16; 3:8). God creates human beings to be in relationship with him.

And he creates them to be in relationship with one another. He creates Adam and Eve for each other, to love one other, to be united with one another (2:24). This, then, is your purpose: to love your spouse, your parents and your children, your neighbour, your enemy, your friends and the community around you. And above this is the call to love God. Jesus confirmed that this is the greatest commandment: to 'love the Lord your God with all your heart and with all your soul and with all your mind,' and that the second greatest is to 'love your neighbour as yourself.'* These are the greatest commandments and your greatest purpose. This is our ultimate and essential purpose, a purpose which will last for eternity.

Therefore, your relationships are your purpose. We are called to love. So, we ask ourselves, not only what we should do, or who we should be, but also who are we supposed to be loving? Who has God put in your life that he is asking you to love?

And so, having arrived in Brazil and trying to work out what I should be doing, the answer which kept coming back to me was that

* Matthew 22:37–39.

my first calling was to love God, and my second was to love Tara and my children. I was to try to make sure that they are my first priority, my first prayers, that they get the best of me and not the leftovers, and then to love all those whom God puts in our path.

LOVE-BE-DO

This is where we start: with the call to love, to be and to do. And the order is important. We are meant to start by being loved, then we discover who we are, and then we work out what to do. Before God commands Adam and Eve to do anything, he blesses them. He loves them before he commands them. He loves them before they know who they are or what they are supposed to do.

This is how childhood is supposed to work, growing up in an atmosphere of love, not able to do anything and not even knowing who we are, but knowing that we are loved. And out of this love we begin to discover our identity and then how best to act. This is what we see in the life of Jesus. He starts just being loved by his Father, affirmed in his identity at his baptism, and only then beginning his ministry. The order is Love-Be-Do.

This is important if we are to ensure that our relationships don't become a means to an end. For example, Tara helps me in countless ways to do the things which I feel that God has called me to do. She also helps me to become the person whom God intended me to be, through encouragements and prayers and confronting my many faults. But there would be something wrong if I was only married to Tara because she helped me fulfil my goals or improve my character. It is important that the relationship exists for its own sake.

This is true of all relationships. If you are friends with someone only to try to achieve something else, and not for the sake of the friendship itself, it will feel transactional or even exploitative. This is true of our relationship with God too. We may start the life of faith loving God because he helps us to do what would otherwise be impossible for us. We may love him because we are aware that he alone enables us to be the people we were always meant to be. But in the end we must find a way of loving God because he is himself lovable, and the relationship is valuable for its own sake.

It is easy for things to go wrong and for the order to be reversed. We start with doing, trying to form an identity by what we do, hoping to become someone who is loved and lovable. We find ourselves stuck in Do-Be-Love. This was a pattern I found myself in at university. Looking back, I think I was trying to do good things to form an identity for myself, so that I would be loved. But it was unsustainable and God in his grace allowed me to get chronic fatigue, taking me back to the start, where I had to learn that I was simply loved by him, that this was my identity, and that anything I should do would flow from this.

If we don't start with love things can fall apart. I have known those who have thrown themselves into their work, even into Christian ministry which seemed so important, but in the process lost themselves and damaged their relationships. I have also known others who were so focused on the attempt to be their authentic selves that they ended up stopping the valuable work they were doing and hurting the people around them.

When Satan tries to ruin the purpose for which Adam and Eve had been made, he doesn't start by trying to get them to do the wrong things. First, he undermines their relationship with God, getting them to doubt God's words and his character. Then he tries to distort their identity, telling them that they need to eat this fruit to become like God.* Instead of being content in who God made them to be, he tells them that they are not enough as they are and promises them that the fruit will give them a new identity which will make them happy. Once he has undermined their relationship with God and distorted their identity, their disobedient actions inevitably follow.

* Genesis 3:1–5.

So, focus first on loving God and you will begin to do the right things. Do not try to form an identity which can be loved. But know that you are loved, and then you will begin to understand who you are. Your greatest purpose is to know the love of God and love him in return. Everything flows from this.

CALLING AND PROVISION

So this is our calling: to love those whom God has given us to love, to be the people God created us to be and to do the things that God gives us to do. And when God calls, he also provides. God blesses Adam and Eve, commanding them to take care of the world, and then he gives them all they need to fulfil their calling. 'Then God said, "I give you every seed-bearing plant on the face of the whole earth and every tree that has fruit with seed in it. They will be yours for food"' (1:29).

God calls and then he provides. In my experience it seems to be almost always in that order. First he calls, then he provides. And he provides for us abundantly and in diverse and beautiful ways. This has been one of the most wonderful things about responding to God's call to Brighton and then to Brazil. We have seen God provide people to help, places to live, and all the finances, the opportunities, the encouragements and the guidance we have needed along the way. God calls us and then gives us the means to fulfil our calling.

God doesn't always give us what we think we need. And he doesn't always give it to us when we think we need it. In the story of the Fall, Satan tempts Adam and Eve to take what they don't need for the wrong calling. But God always provides what we do need to fulfil what he has asked us to do, and to be the people he wants us to be, and to love those he has given to us to love.

Adam and Eve failed in this calling. And we will always fail to live out our calling perfectly. Instead of doing what God wants us to do, we find ourselves battling with frustration. Instead of being the people God made us to be, we live in confusion. Instead of loving those God has given us to love, we very often struggle with isolation and complicated relationships.

However, God has sent his Son into the world, and 'the Son is the image of the invisible God, the firstborn over all creation.'* He is the only one who has ever done exactly what he should have been doing, the only one who was and is perfectly who he was meant to be, and the only one who perfectly loved those he was called to love. He is the most beautiful of all images. On the cross it appeared that he had failed, that he had been disfigured, that he was unloved, when, in reality, it was a display of total victory: his true identity confirmed and perfect love revealed. And we are being transformed into his likeness. The Holy Spirit is at work within every Christian, to enable us to do what God wants us to do, to be the people he made us to be and to love those he is calling us to love.

We arrived in Rio in August 2022 without a plan. We believed that our presence here was intrinsically valuable, whether or not we managed to achieve anything at all. We would try to love each other, love the people around us, and most importantly love God, trying to spend as much time with him as possible. We spent a lot of time quoting, 'We do not know what to do, but our eyes are on you.'** From this basis we hoped that we would be able to take hold of whatever adventure God sent our way.

* Colossians 1:15.
** 2 Chronicles 20:12.

PART TWO

Discovery

Chapter 3

GOING

Abraham
Genesis 12:1–13

---

*The LORD had said to Abram, 'Go from your country, your people
and your father's household to the land I will show you.*

> *'I will make you into a great nation,
> and I will bless you;
> I will make your name great,
> and you will be a blessing.
> I will bless those who bless you,
> and whoever curses you I will curse;
> and all peoples on earth
> will be blessed through you.'*

GENESIS 12:1–3

Go to them. Go as far as you can. Loving the Lord your God, and
your neighbour. That's what the whole thing is about.

JACKIE PULLINGER*

It all starts with the voice of God. At the very start of the Bible, God
speaks and the world is created. And here in Genesis 12, God speaks
and Abraham's purpose is created. Our calling begins with the voice
of God. It is not simply the voice within – our own ideas, desires,
hopes and dreams – though of course God loves them and is able
to work with them, and God often places ideas, passions and hopes

---

* Jackie Pullinger, 'An interview with Jackie Pullinger', *HTB at Home*, 14 February
2021, youtube.com (accessed May 2024).

in our hearts. Nor is it the voices around us – the expectations of others, the assumptions of our culture, the views of our family and friends – though God can work through these too. It is the voice from above which breaks into our lives and takes primacy over all other voices. Therefore, we start with the God who speaks to us, trying to recognize the voice of God and follow it over our internal impulses, or the instinct to follow the crowd around us.

And God calls us, saying: 'Go.' God calls Abraham, saying: 'Go', to leave behind the people he knows and place he knows. The command 'Go' is one of the most frequent commands that God gives to his people in the Old Testament, and it is one of the most frequent commands that Jesus gives to his disciples in the New Testament. It is the first command that God gives when he begins to call individuals at the beginning of Genesis, and it is the last command that Jesus gives to his disciples in Matthew's Gospel.* Ultimately, we are called to 'Go' because this is the example which God himself gives to us, for Jesus left heaven and came into the world for our sake. Jesus fulfilled his purpose by going and calls us to fulfil our purpose by going. Therefore, being open to the call of God means being prepared to go.

God is always asking us to go. Sometimes 'going' will be dramatic and obvious, at other times it will be more subtle and hidden, but we are always supposed to go. Sometimes we are called to go to new places; at other times it is to new people, new activities or new ways of operating. There have been moments in my life when 'going' has meant big moves to a new city and a new country. There have been other times when it has meant going to a neighbourhood I would normally avoid, or to go and talk to someone whom I've noticed and felt prompted to approach.

God says to Abram, 'Go from your country' (12:1). It is a call to leave the environment that he knew, the place that was familiar and safe. He tells Abram to leave his people (12:1), to let go of the relationships that had held him and defined him. And he commands him to leave his father's household (12:1), which suggests letting go

* Matthew 28:19.

of a lifestyle he'd got used to. He is being asked to leave behind his home, his culture, his relationships and his lifestyle, exchanging what was known for what was unknown, what was familiar with what was unfamiliar.

Going always means leaving something behind. And it was not a small thing for Abraham to leave Ur behind. Ur was in Mesopotamia, in the Fertile Crescent between the great rivers, the Tigris and the Euphrates. Mesopotamia was the birthplace of many of the basic aspects of human civilization, where agriculture was invented, irrigation was first developed and where the very earliest evidence of human sedentary settlement has been found. The first cities were formed here. And at the time of Abram, it was probably unified as the first regional state, with Ur at the centre.

Ur was founded in about 3800 BC and had existed for almost 2000 years by the time of Abram. Possibly 60,000 people were living there, which was vast by the standards of the day. It was surrounded by thousands of hectares of land producing dates, sesame and cereals, and hundreds more dedicated to dairy farming and sheep herding. There were fish farms and reed factories, artisan operations in the city producing pottery and reed-work, and it had massive temple architecture dominating the centre of the city. It was a centre of learning and culture, where 'three of the most important social technologies in the history of human civilization' were invented: literacy, numeracy and accounting.* This was perhaps the most exciting place in the world to live. I imagine it wasn't easy to leave all of this behind.

When Tara and I sensed this call to go from the UK to Brazil it was not something we had expected. I really like England. I love the mild climate, the non-threatening wildlife, the stony beaches, cricket and BBC Radio 4. And we loved our city of Brighton and our church there. But God called us to go. And that meant leaving things behind. In those first few months after we had moved to Rio de Janeiro, Tara and I became very conscious of all that we had left,

---

* Felix Martin, *Money: The Unauthorised Biography* (Bodley Head, 2013), pp38–39.

our house, our country, a job, the children's school, and most of all our community, the feeling of belonging, being in a place where we were known and loved and wanted.

God makes it sound so simple – he simply tells him to 'go'. But for Abram, going will involve not only leaving so much behind but also facing all kinds of challenges and complications: travelling to Canaan, visiting Egypt, the outbreak of disease, conflict with Pharoah, falling out with his nephew Lot, war, kidnapping, rescue, meeting strange people, long periods of waiting, tests and trials.* It is not easy to go. But as we respond to what God is calling us to go to, we begin to see some beautiful things which would never have happened otherwise.

EXPERIENCING BLESSING

First, God blesses us as we go. God was asking Abram to give up so much, but God called him so that he could bless him. God demands everything of us, but only so that he can give back to us even more. The words 'bless' or 'blessing' occur five times in just two verses (12:2–3). God calls us so that he can bless us.

God is always longing to pour into our lives his goodness and his grace, his healing and forgiveness, his comfort and his provision, his affirmation and his truth. But our natural tendency is to build up our lives in ways which block his blessing. We work out ways to make ourselves secure and so we don't need his protection. We ensure that we always have enough and so don't need his provision. We get our 'likes' from social media and so don't need his affirmation. We have already worked out our plans and so don't need his guidance. But when we go, everything changes. Suddenly we need his comfort and his provision, his wisdom and direction, and God begins to bless us in ways we had never known before. God calls us to go so that he can bless us.

I held on to this conviction tightly in those early months in Rio de Janeiro, when we were aware of all that we had left behind: God had promised to bless us, and so he would bless us in this unfamiliar land.

* Genesis 12 – 23.

29

And as we go, we become a blessing to others too. Going can have an extraordinary impact on the places and people we go to. For our calling is ultimately not about us. It is not for our fulfilment, but for the sake of the world that God loves. We are to go because God loves the people we are being sent to, and because God loves the places he commands us to go to. He wants to bless us, and he wants to bless others through us.

GROWING CLOSER

Second, we grow closer to God as we go, as we learn to trust him in new ways. Abram goes and soon after starts calling on the name of the Lord (13:4). We don't hear of Abram doing this before he goes, but once he goes, perhaps because he knows he needs to, he begins to call on the name of the Lord. One of his first actions is to build an altar so that he can worship God (12:7). So much has been removed, and he knows that he has nothing else.

This relationship with God grows as Abram goes. Chapter 12 starts with God *speaking* to Abram, but after he goes to Canaan, it says that God *appeared* to Abram (12:7). There is a growth in intimacy and in his experience of God's presence. As he responds to God's call, he begins to experience the presence of God in a new way.

When we arrived in Rio, we had little idea of what we were supposed to be doing here. We had no plan, or strategy, or even much of a vision. We didn't even know how we were going to get through each day. So we started calling on the name of the Lord. Each morning we gathered whoever was around to pray. Then we quickly increased it to three times a day. We might not have known *what* we were doing, but we could get to know the one *who* had called us, and we would call on his name for everything we needed.

BEING TRANSFORMED

Third, God transforms us as we go. God commands Abram to go, and then promises to make him into a great nation (12:2). He will be transformed as he goes. Like all of us, he has not yet become who God means for him to be, but as he goes God will enable him to be the one that he is calling him to be. Later, after he has entered the land of Canaan, he will even be given a new name, 'Abraham' (17:5). We are not yet those whom God has called us to be, but as we go, he works within us, transforming us, reshaping us and renaming us.

ENCOUNTERING DIFFICULTY

Fourth, when we go, we go into difficulty. Abram goes in obedience to God, travelling huge distances, and then immediately we read, 'Now there was a famine in the land' (12:10).

Responding to the call of God is not a guarantee of an easy life. Quite the opposite. Our first year in Rio de Janeiro was one of the hardest we have ever been through, with all kinds of problems that we never anticipated. There were times when Tara and I asked one another whether we would have said 'yes' if we had known what it was going to be like. Our second year was not much easier.

Obedience to God's call doesn't shield us from problems. Nor does it hide our weaknesses. More often it exposes our weaknesses. When they face a famine, Abram loses his nerve and they move to Egypt. Then, when he gets there, he starts to pretend that his wife is not really his wife. In the stories which follow their obedience to God's call, all Abram and Sarai's character flaws seem to come to the surface: their fears, deception, lack of faith, impatience and jealousy. As we go, our weaknesses are often brought to the surface, particularly in our relationships.

In those first few months in Rio, it felt like so many of my weaknesses were becoming visible, my failings as a husband and a father, my desire to be liked and popular in the church, my fear of criticism and sensitivity if people didn't like the things we were doing. I became more aware than ever of my own idolatries and insecurities which might have remained hidden had we stayed in England.

As we go, we often feel much weaker. But we also experience God's power. As they respond to God's call, Abram and Sarai go through some difficult and painful experiences, but they also see miracles, with angels appearing, and extraordinary provision and protection taking place. There are daring rescues, fire from heaven, miraculous births and promises fulfilled. And for us, these first few years in Rio have brought more dramatic answers to prayer than we had ever seen before. Refusing to go might hide our weaknesses and shield us from some problems, but it might also hide God's power. But as we respond to God's call both our weaknesses and his power become more evident.

MOVING AND SETTLING

And so we go, taking the first step in response to God's call. God doesn't tell Abram the whole plan, just the next step. We rarely get to see the whole picture, only what we need to do next. That's certainly how we felt when we were trying to move to Brazil. When people asked what we were going to do there, what the plan was or to share the vision, the only reply we had was, 'We are just trying to get to Brazil.' We were simply trying to take the first step. A boat can only be steered when it is moving, and in the same way it is harder to sense God's guidance if we're not moving. For this reason, fear, apathy and cynicism are dangerous obstacles to a life of purpose: they stop us from moving.

Then, once we start going, there are two temptations. The first is to settle too quickly. We know from the book of Acts that God called Abram while he was still in Ur. Abram left Ur to travel to Canaan with his father, Terah,* but they stopped when they arrived in Harran.** Harran is about halfway to Canaan. They had got stuck along the way. They had stopped moving. We can set off with a vision, a sense of what God wants us to do, but we can get stuck

* Genesis 11:31.
** Acts 7:4.

along the way. We settle too quickly, losing sight of what God has asked us to do.

The second temptation is to become rootless, failing to settle in the place God has called us to live. God had called Abram to settle in Canaan, but almost immediately, at the first sign of difficulty, he moves to Egypt, away from the land God had called him. The process of moving involves the cutting of so many ties, letting go of those things which have rooted us in a particular place, we can find it difficult to re-establish these in a new place, becoming rootless and detached. But God often calls us not just to go, but to settle; not just to move but to move in.

The call to 'go' is not the call to drift, to avoid commitments or to give up and run away when things get tough. We are called to go and then stay. As we prepared to move from the UK some friends told us the story of a missionary who went to see his mentor when he had arrived in Africa. He told his mentor of his five aims for his first year as a missionary. But his mentor stopped him and said to him, 'You have only one aim for your first year. That is to still be here.' We thought of this story many times in our first year in Brazil: our aim was simply still to be here by the end of the first year. As the missionary, Jackie Pullinger, put it, 'We need people who will go, and to stay until the end.'

Being called involves both the big moments, when we make life-changing decisions, willing to risk everything and change everything in response to God's voice, and (more frequently) the smaller, everyday moments, just living in a place, trying to be good and kind, and loving the people around us.

GOING TOGETHER

And we work it out together. God calls Abram to go with Sarai. Abram and Sarai set out together, even though it appears, at this stage, as if God has only spoken to Abram. But what about Sarai's purpose? Does she just have to go along with whatever purpose God has for her husband?

Our calling is never simply about our individual purpose, but working out how we can help one another with whatever God has called each person to do. If you don't yet know what to do with your life, if you don't yet have a vision for what you should be doing, then look around and see who does, and attach yourself to them and do everything you can to help them.

We see this again and again in the Bible. Sarai went with Abram and helped him fulfil his purpose of entering the land of Canaan. Aaron and Miriam helped Moses in the work of liberating and leading God's people out of Egypt and into the Promised Land. Barak helped Deborah win a victory against the Israelites' oppressors. Baruch helped Jeremiah in his work as a prophet. Mordecai helped Esther fulfil her calling of rescuing the Jewish people from destruction in Persia. And Joseph went with Mary and helped her to fulfil her purpose of being mother to the Son of God. Sometimes helping another to fulfil their purpose comes at great cost for the one who helps, as it did for Jonathan, the eldest son of King Saul and heir to the throne, who devoted his life to help his friend David to become king instead of him and lost his life in the process.

For many years we felt called to help Archie and Sam Coates lead St Peter's in Brighton. There were many aspects of the work there which we felt passionate about and called to, but we were also there because Archie and Sam came to Brighton with a vision, and we decided that we were going to stick with them and help them to fulfil God's calling on their lives. And a significant part of our move to Rio de Janeiro for me was the conviction that God had called Tara here and my role was to help her to fulfil her calling.

The Christian life is not about you trying to find your purpose on your own, nor is it about trying to persuade other people to help you to fulfil your purpose. We are to help one another with each one's calling. If you are married, you are meant to help your husband or wife to discover and fulfil their purpose. If you have children, it is to help them to fulfil their purpose. If you have friends or work colleagues, it is not a question of how they can help you fulfil your purpose but how you can help them fulfil theirs. If you're a pastor, the congregation does not exist to help you with your purpose, but you are there to help them fulfil theirs.

Later, God would speak to Sarai too, but first she had to trust that God had spoken to Abram and go with him. She may have felt she was only doing this for her husband. However, God was working through her willingness to go with her husband to give her what she wanted more than anything else: to have a son. And that is what she later received. She went with Abram when he felt that it was time to go, and later God gave her the desires of her heart. If you want to receive the things that you feel most passionate about, then maybe start by looking around and helping those around you to fulfil their purpose, until God speaks to you about yours.

PITCHING TENTS AND BUILDING ALTARS

It is easy to lose heart along the way. We can look around at what other people are doing and begin to conform to their lives or their expectations of us. We can find ourselves giving into our natural desires for comfort, affirmation or security, basing our lives on these instead of listening to the voice of God. Abram and Sarai make many mistakes along the way, but they continue to worship God through it all, and God continues to be with them, guiding and protecting them and helping them to fulfil their callings.

When Abram arrives in the land God is giving to him, he pitches a tent and builds an altar (12:8). And he continued to live like this in the land. This is a picture of how we are supposed to live. The places we live, the lifestyles we adopt, the things we do – our tents – are flexible and always changing as we respond to the call of God. But our worship and devotion to Jesus – our altars – they are permanent and solid and consistent. We are called to pitch tents and build altars. Where and how we live may change; whom we devote our lives to is unchanging.

Chapter 4

GROWING

Joseph
Genesis 37–50

---

*Joseph had a dream, and when he told it to his brothers, they
hated him all the more. He said to them, 'Listen to this dream
I had: We were binding sheaves of grain out in the field when
suddenly my sheaf rose and stood upright, while your sheaves
gathered round mine and bowed down to it.'*

GENESIS 37:5–7

*Joseph said to his brothers, 'I am Joseph! Is my father still living?'
But his brothers were not able to answer him, because they were
terrified at his presence.*

*Then Joseph said to his brothers, 'Come close to me.' When they
had done so, he said, 'I am your brother Joseph, the one you sold
into Egypt! And now, do not be distressed and do not be angry
with yourselves for selling me here, because it was to save lives
that God sent me ahead of you.'*

GENESIS 45:3–5

The world needs dreamers and the world needs doers. But most
of all the world needs dreamers who do.

SARAH BAN BREATHNACH*

---

* Sarah Ban Breathnach, *Simple Abundance: 365 Days to a Balanced and Joyful Life*
(Hachette, 1995), September 7.

God calls us and sends us. But it might not always feel like it, and we might not feel that we are making any choices along the way. For most of Joseph's life, he would not have felt like he had much choice. As a teenager his father, Jacob, sends him to see his brothers. Then his brothers throw him into a cistern, and he is taken against his will into Egypt, where he is sold to Potiphar, then put in prison, before being summoned to Pharoah's court.* For most of his life he has had very little freedom in what he does or where he goes. And yet his purpose remains, and at the end of his story Joseph will say, 'God sent me' (45:7).

Our calling emerges from a combination of choice and necessity, the few things we choose to do, and many other things about which we have no choice. For most people, at most times, there is very little choice about where we live or what we do, and our lives are formed around the obligations of family and society: children who need to be provided for, parents who need to be cared for and the need to survive. Our location, our work, our activities and even our relationships are usually formed by necessity rather than choice. Joseph does what his father asks of him, and then he does as he is told by those who have power over him. Similarly, very often we are simply responding to the needs of our families and the restraints of our environment.

And yet, even when we feel like we have very little freedom to shape the direction of our lives, God's purposes are being fulfilled through it all. God is at work in both the choices and the necessity. Joseph may have felt like he had little or no choice, that other people were always in control, but by the end he knows that God sent him.

GROWING IN CHARACTER

God fulfils his purpose through the development of Joseph's character. Purpose requires both inspiration and character. God's call on our lives often starts with him speaking to us, inspiring us and giving us

* Genesis 37; 39; 41.

dreams and visions about what might be possible. But inspiration on its own is not enough. We may have dreams and visions and be filled with inspiration, but a life of purpose is one where vision becomes action and inspiration moves to implementation, where our dreams become a reality. And the bridge between our dreams and the fulfilment of our dreams is our character. For it is one thing to have dreams, it is another to have the character to fulfil them.

The story of Joseph begins with him aged seventeen and having dreams, but he lacks the character to fulfil these dreams. He is self-obsessed, unwise, lacking self-control, unkind and brings the worst out of the people around him. But then he goes through a series of terrible experiences. He is seized by his brothers and sold into slavery in Egypt. He works for Potiphar in Egypt and does well, being promoted and managing the whole household, but then he faces temptation when Potiphar's wife tries to seduce him. He is accused of attempted rape by Potiphar's wife and thrown into prison. He works hard there and is again promoted so that he is running the prison. During that time two other prisoners tell him of their dreams, which they had each had one night. He correctly interprets their dreams, and one of them is freed, promising to remember Joseph and help him, but he fails to do this for another two years. Finally, Pharaoh has two dreams and Joseph is called from prison to interpret them, which he does successfully. Pharaoh realizes his wisdom and capability, making Joseph ruler over Egypt, responsible for the task of protecting Egypt from the famine which his dreams had foretold. He becomes responsible not only for this fifteen-year project to feed Egypt and the surrounding area, but also given authority over the whole of Egypt. He's just thirty years old.

Then, after seven years of good harvests, the famine begins to take hold. After a couple of years his brothers come down from Canaan to buy food. They bow down before the new ruler of Egypt and, after some tests which he sets for them, Joseph reveals who he is. He is reconciled to his brothers and then his father. It's about twenty years since he had his dreams and they are finally being fulfilled.

The story of Joseph is one of inspiration becoming reality through the development of character. At the start of the story, he is a teenager with great dreams. He is inspired. And the story ends with his dreams becoming a reality. But in between the dreams and the fulfilment of his dreams is the formation of Joseph's character. God gives Joseph some dreams, and then he begins to form his character so that those dreams can be fulfilled.

So often we ask God what we should be doing, when God seems to be more interested in who we are becoming. We might ask God where we should be going, but God is more interested in how we are growing. For God not only gives us inspiration, dreams and visions, but also gets to work on our characters, forming us into the people who can fulfil these visions.

The development of our characters rarely happens without pain. Joseph goes through the relational pain of rejection, betrayal and isolation. He experiences professional pain, being falsely accused, unjustly imprisoned and enslaved by those he worked for. And he goes through spiritual pain, with years of waiting for his God-given dreams to be fulfilled, having his hopes raised and then dashed. It is a cycle of constant disappointment and delay.

Our lives often turn out very differently from what we expect. Joseph had dreams as a teenager, but the reality of his life seemed so different. It was far harder, but also far more significant, than he could have predicted. For through all this God was forming his character and enabling him to become the person to fulfil his purposes.

Looking at the example of Joseph, there seem to be four main ways in which God grows our character, so that we can fulfil our purpose: Integrity, Wisdom, Belonging and Service.

GROWING IN INTEGRITY

First, God enables us to grow in integrity. When Joseph reveals himself to his brothers he says, 'I am Joseph!' (45:3). This is not only a statement of his identity but also an affirmation that through the years he has not lost sight of who he is.

The high point of some of the greatest books and films I grew up with was the moment when the character revealed their name. In *Les Miserables*, the police inspector Javert calls the escaped prisoner turned mayor Jean Valjean, 'Prisoner 24601', but the hero insists, 'My name is Jean Valjean.'* In *The Matrix*, Agent Smith says to the character played by Keanu Reeves, 'Goodbye, Mr Anderson' and he replies, 'My name is Neo.'** Or in *Gladiator*, Emperor Commodus says to Russell Crowe's gladiator, 'Slave. You will remove your helmet and tell me your name,' and the gladiator turns and says, 'My name is Maximus Decimus Meridius, commander of the Armies of the North, general of the Felix Legions, loyal servant to the true emperor, Marcus Aurelius, father to a murdered son, husband to a murdered wife and I will have my vengeance, in this life or the next.'***

In this story we have a similarly dramatic moment, where the Egyptian chief administrator turns to the Hebrews and says, 'I am Joseph!' This is particularly striking because throughout the story, as it is written in Genesis, almost none of the other characters ever call Joseph by his name or even refer to him by his name.**** His brothers call him 'that dreamer' (37:19), 'our brother' (37:26) or 'the boy' (37:30). To Potiphar and his wife, Joseph is 'this Hebrew' (39:14) or 'that Hebrew slave' (39:17). In prison he is described as 'a young Hebrew … a servant' (41:12). Pharaoh gives him a new name, 'Zaphenath-Paneah' (41:45), and then finally he becomes known as 'ruler of all Egypt' (45:8).

He has been through so much. He has had failures and successes, and he hasn't been called by his real name for twenty years, and yet

* Claude-Michel Schönberg, *Les Miserables: a Musical* (H Leonard, 1988).
** L Wachowski & L Wachowski, *The Matrix* (Warner Bros, 1999).
*** Ridley Scott, *Gladiator* (Dreamworks, 2000).
**** Only once, in Genesis 41:55, does Pharaoh refer to Joseph by name, and that is only in his absence.

he has never lost his sense of who he is. He is not 'the slave'. He is not a victim. He is not defined by his nationality or by his race. He is not defined by his position, or by the opinions of other people. He is not defined by his past failures or present successes. He lets suffering transform him but not define him. He is simply Joseph. Through it all he knows who he is.

Perhaps it was his father's love which secured him and defined him throughout his life. This father loved him genuinely and abundantly, but imperfectly. But we have a heavenly Father who loves us genuinely, eternally and perfectly, and he is the one who defines us and affirms us, and who ensures that we never forget who we are.

GROWING IN WISDOM

Second, God enables us to grow in wisdom. Wisdom is the art of living well. It is doing the right thing at the right time in the right way. It is self-control, self-discipline and effective action, bringing out the best in the people around you and acting with honesty and foresight.

At the beginning of his story, Joseph lacks wisdom. He brings a bad report to his father about his brothers (37:2). He lacks self-control, unable to resist telling his brothers about the dreams he was having about ruling over them (37:6–9). In the opening verses he frequently speaks but rarely listens (37:2–9). He seems to bring out the worst in the people around him, rather than the best.

However, by the end of the story he has moved from doing what he wants to do to doing what is right. He resists the temptation to sleep with Potiphar's wife, fleeing from a situation in which he could be compromised (39:12). Interestingly, he doesn't say to Potiphar's wife that it is not something he wants. He tells her that it's not right (39:9). He may well have been attracted to her. He could even have been in love with her, but he knew it was not right, so he avoided her and fled from her when she tried to seduce him.

At the start his brothers are more often the workers and he is more often the observer, sent to see how they are getting on and report back on them (37:12–14). He is a dreamer more than a doer. But he moves from being unpractical to being practical. In every place he finds himself he gets to work, becoming more organized and efficient at getting things done. Despite everything that Joseph has experienced, he does not become helpless or passive and nor does he give up. In every situation he works hard and makes the best of the opportunities which present themselves to him.

This is wisdom: doing what is good, right and effective. And this is essential for fulfilling our purpose. We need to be people of action and not just rhetoric; practice and not just theory; not just people of vision, but people who enable vision to become reality.

GROWING IN BELONGING

Third, God develops our capacity for belonging, which is the ability to be close to other people, to love and be loved.

Joseph is repeatedly hurt, rejected and mistreated by those who should have looked after him. He was favoured by his father in ways which spoilt him and alienated him from his siblings (37:3–4). He is hated and then sold by his brothers into slavery (37:4, 28). He is falsely accused by his employer's wife (39:17–18) and then forgotten by a fellow prisoner who promised to help him (40:23). When you've been hurt so often in relationships, as Joseph was, it is natural to become hardened, to withdraw and keep people at a distance, or to retaliate and hurt those who hurt you. We often want them to feel bad, and for everyone to know how badly they have treated us. And we lose empathy, for it often feels impossible to make space for the pain of others when we are in pain ourselves.

But Joseph shows empathy for the baker and cupbearer he meets in prison. And when he reveals himself to his brothers, instead of making them feel bad, Joseph says, 'Do not be angry with yourselves' (45:5). Instead of keeping them at a distance, he says to them, 'Come close to me' (45:4) and embraces them (45:14–15).

Instead of ensuring everyone knows their faults, he protects their reputation, ordering his attendants to leave (45:1). And he refuses to make them suffer as he had, for whilst everything was taken from him, he gives generously to those who had hurt him (45:21–23). He chooses kindness over retaliation. And his heart has remained soft, for he weeps with his brothers (45:2).

As a teenager he is isolated, unkind and brings out hostility from those around him. Here he is connected, compassionate and brings out the best in his brothers. Through everything that he's gone through he has grown in empathy, grown in kindness and grown in love.

The toughest things we go through in life are often the things that teach us to love: softening our hearts, teaching us empathy, enabling us to be close to other people. I have had many moments in my life when I have felt a connection with someone I'm talking to, wondering what it is, and then I find out that they've gone through some kind of crisis: a breakdown, a broken heart, a bereavement, and I've realized that the experience has created for this person a softness and an ability to connect at a deeper level.

GROWING IN SERVICE

Fourth, God grows our ability to serve, which is where we stop making our lives about ourselves.

Joseph starts this story being self-obsessed, but he ends by being focused on what God is doing and on the needs of others. When he was a teenager, his dreams were about himself. And they are perhaps not unusual things for us to dream about when we are teenagers: being powerful, popular and successful. Essentially, they are dreams about becoming a celebrity, with everyone bowing down to him. But, by the end, he is serving a great nation, working hard and using all his gifts to enable them to avoid famine. He has grown in practical skills and people management, starting with a household, then progressing to a prison, before overseeing an entire nation.

And through all of this, Joseph learns that his life is not about himself. During his years of waiting Joseph has to deal with other people telling him about their dreams, whilst his own dreams have remained unfulfilled. It must have been so painful to have been reminded of his own unfulfilled dreams so often. It must have been tempting to say to other people, 'Don't talk to me about dreams! Dreams are never fulfilled. Dreams only disappoint and lead to pain and rejection.' But as he grows in character, he stops focusing on his own dreams. He moves from his own personal dreams to interpreting the dreams of others. Instead of thinking about his own place and role, he is thinking about others.

Then, when his dreams are finally fulfilled, he tells his brothers that their actions were all part, not of the fulfilment of his dreams, but of God's plan for 'the saving of many lives' (50:20). It seems like his own role in all this has become irrelevant to him.

Andrea Jaeger was the world-number-two tennis player in the 1980s. She reached the French Open final in 1982 and the final of Wimbledon in 1983. After she retired from tennis, she set up charities for children and eventually became a Dominican nun. She was once asked by the great tennis player and commentator John McEnroe, 'How do you want to be remembered?' And she replied, 'I don't have to be remembered. I do what I am called to do because I am called to do it. Not so that I am remembered.'*

At the end of Genesis, Joseph makes his descendants promise to take his bones to Canaan after he dies. I find this interesting, because I imagine that Egypt had some good options for the burials of their rulers, like massive pyramids! Though he was surrounded by these extraordinary monuments to their leaders, Joseph decides he wants to be buried with the rest of his family and ancestors in the obscurity of Canaan. It's not about him anymore. Sometimes God is just waiting for us to stop making

* Terence Handley MacMath, 'Interview: Andrea Jaeger Former Tennis Star, Now a Religious in the US Episcopal Church' *The Church Times*, 6 June 2008, churchtimes.co.uk (accessed May 2024).

our lives all about us, so that he can fulfil his purposes through us. Paul writes, 'live a life worthy of the calling you have received.'* It is not a command to find a great and worthy calling. Instead, the assumption is that we are called, and now we are to grow in the character which fits such a calling.

What is it that causes the growth of Joseph's character in this way, when others may have gone through similar experiences but become more self-obsessed, bitter and dysfunctional in their relationships? It seems that it is his confidence in the purposes of God. Three times Joseph tells his brothers, 'God sent me' (45:5, 7, 8). It was not his own sense of purpose that kept him going, but his confidence in God's purposes. He knew that God was at work in his life, through both the trials and the successes.

Joseph's faith is particularly impressive when we notice that God is hidden in so much of his story. In the stories we read of his father, Jacob, grandfather, Isaac and great-grandfather, Abraham, God makes visible appearances, speaks audibly, sends angels and wrestles them by rivers. With Joseph we find none of these kinds of divine appearances or interventions. He has some dreams but no clear voice from God. There are dreams which come from God, but they need interpretation. He would have grown up hearing about these dramatic stories, but doesn't get to experience any of them himself, and yet he remains confident that God is at work in hidden and indirect ways.

This is the character which God grows in us as he calls us: integrity, wisdom, belonging and service. The story of Joseph points us to one who would come many years later, who was also betrayed and condemned, and who would be perfect in every aspect of his character: Jesus Christ, perfect in integrity because he is the great I AM, perfect in belonging, for he is Love himself, the perfect Wisdom of God and the faultless Suffering Servant, who fulfilled his perfect purpose by being the perfect person who loved the Father perfectly.

* Ephesians 4:1.

Chapter 5

DRAWING NEAR

Moses
Exodus 3:1 – 4:18

———————————

*But Moses said to God, 'Who am I that I should go to Pharaoh
and bring the Israelites out of Egypt?'*
EXODUS 3:11

Now, Bree, you poor, proud, frightened Horse, draw near.
Nearer still, my son. Do not dare not to dare. Touch me. Smell
me. Here are my paws, here is my tail, these are my whiskers.
I am a true Beast.

THE HORSE AND HIS BOY*

When one of our children was around two years old, she would get
two books from the bookshelf in her room at bedtime, and then
crawl up into my lap, handing me one of the books and asking me
to read to her. I would start to read, at which point she would get
the other book and start 'reading' it at the same time (although
she hadn't yet learnt to read and was only making up the words). I
would then stop and listen to her, but she would insist that I carry
on reading the first story. So we would both be reading our stories
in competition.

This is a picture of how our calling often seems to work. It starts
by crawling into the lap of the Father. It emerges from intimacy with
the one who has loved us from the start, who knows us completely
and who wants good things for us. As we do this, God starts to read

* CS Lewis, *The Horse and his Boy* (HarperCollins, 2023), p213.

to us the story of our lives, beginning to guide us, shape how we live and mould us into who we are meant to be.

This is how the call of Moses begins. He goes to Horeb, the mountain of God (Exodus 3:1), entering the place of God's presence. He sees a bush on fire which does not burn up and decides to take a closer look. As he moves towards God, he moves towards his calling. A bush on fire might not have been particularly unusual, but its failure to burn up was. Moses meets with God through witnessing something both ordinary and extraordinary, something which combined the mundane and the miraculous. This is a picture of the Christian life: so much of life feels normal and unexceptional, but mixed in with it are elements which are beyond the normal, which seem to bear the handprint of God himself.

Next, Moses hears God's voice, and responds by taking off his sandals. Moses was a shepherd, supposedly looking after his father-in-law's sheep, but he is beginning to discover something more important than sheep. His focus has moved away from his flock to this strange sight. He has removed his sandals, which I imagine were quite useful when working as a shepherd in a stony desert landscape, and his full attention is now on the one who is calling him. He is taking a break from his normal working life to meet with God, and in doing so will have his life turned around.

Our calling emerges in relationship with God; it is in the presence of God that he begins to read us the story of our lives. However, like my daughter, we then go off and get our own books and try to read our own story at the same time. As a result, we find ourselves with two different stories competing for dominance: the story that God wants to read over us, and the story that we would like for ourselves. It is the battle between what we want for our lives and what God wants to do in us and through us. It is a battle between what we would naturally choose and what God is inviting us to choose.

This is the dynamic in which Moses finds himself. Before Moses had this life-changing encounter with God at the burning bush, he might already have had a sense of purpose for his life: to build up his flocks, make progress in his work for his father-in-law, have a happy family, get his kids into the best Midianite schools, and avoid too much disruption and discomfort. But God meets with Moses through this burning bush, and it is here that God reveals that he has another story for Moses, a greater purpose: to go down to Egypt, confront Pharaoh, liberate an enslaved people and lead them into a new land.

There is often a battle between our hopes and dreams for our lives and God's hopes and dreams for our lives. We might have big plans, we might be dreaming of success, celebrity and wealth, but God has something far bigger and better for us; maybe not by the standards of the world around us, but certainly greater than the story we would write for ourselves. Often it will feel like an internal struggle between what we want and what God wants, and it can be difficult to embrace a different plan to the one we had for ourselves and to trust that God has a better and more beautiful story for us to become a part.

This new story emerges as we draw close to the living God. We begin to let go of our plans and embrace God's plans, leaving behind what we would have chosen and trusting in what he has chosen for us. We start placing our lives, our stories, our hopes and our dreams in God's hands, and we align ourselves with the story that God has for us.

OPEN TO DISRUPTION

When God calls us, it can often feel like an interruption, or even a disruption, to our lives. For God speaks to us and redirects our lives in ways we were not expecting or planning. Therefore, if we close ourselves off from interruption, we are in danger of closing ourselves off from God's call. Here, Moses was not apparently looking for a career change. He was not asking to be called. God's call was unplanned, unexpected and unsought. He was simply going about his work when God interrupted his plans for this life.

Both the big moves in my life have come as interruptions. I had no plan to leave London in my early twenties, but one conversation with a friend in 2008 sparked a change of direction which would see us move to Brighton and remain there for the next thirteen years. We soon felt settled in Brighton and didn't imagine ever moving from there, but then a tiny thought sparked a longer conversation and suddenly we were off to Brazil. God's call is disruptive. It changes the way we work, where we live, whom we love and serve and how we spend our time.

It can start with something very small. For Moses it was a little curiosity to see why a bush was on fire but not burning up, and for us it can start with a tiny thought, a question or a conversation in which we allow God to start disrupting our lives.

REMEMBERING WHO WE ARE

As we meet with God, he reminds us of who we are supposed to be. When God calls out, 'Moses! Moses!' from the burning bush (Genesis 3:4), he is not only getting Moses' attention, he is also reminding Moses of who he is. Moses has lost his purpose because he has forgotten who he is.

'Moses', though probably an Egyptian name, sounds like the Hebrew for 'draw out', and was given to him because of the way in which he was rescued (2:10). He was an Israelite, born when God's people were living in slavery in Egypt. Pharaoh had given an order to kill all Hebrew baby boys, but Moses' mother had hidden her child in a basket, and he had been saved from the water by Pharaoh's daughter. She had given him this name, a reminder that he had been rescued.

And he was rescued so that he could become a rescuer. There was something deep within Moses which wanted to rescue people. Three times already he had tried to intervene to rescue those in trouble: a Hebrew slave being beaten by his Egyptian slavedriver (2:11–12), two Hebrew slaves fighting each other (2:13) and the daughters of Reuel when they were driven away by local shepherds (2:17).

Deep within, Moses was a rescuer, but he couldn't see this in himself anymore. It's a reminder that God sees us more clearly than we see ourselves. He knows who we are when we have forgotten our identity, and he is always seeking to reveal to us, or to remind us, who we are so that he can restore our purpose. God reminds Moses that, even though he has run to the other side of the desert, he is still *Moses*.

Jesus begins his ministry with the words of his Father reminding him of who he is: 'You are my Son, whom I love; with you I am well pleased.' Satan will try to steer him off course by getting him to forget his identity three times, in two of them explicitly questioning it, saying to him, 'If you are the Son of God …' but his identity remains secure. And this is the launchpad for the purpose of his life.*

It is the same for us. As God calls us, he reminds us of who we are.

CONNECTING TO OUR CONTEXT

But God also gets us to think beyond ourselves. He connects us to our contexts. God tells Moses, 'I have indeed seen the misery of my people in Egypt. I have heard them crying out because of their slave drivers, and I am concerned about their suffering' (3:7). God is reminding Moses of the injustice which the Israelites are enduring in Egypt. It seems that Moses has tried to disconnect himself from the oppression he had seen in Egypt, but God now wants to reconnect him to his context. As God speaks to Moses, he steers him away from thinking about himself, his skills and desires, and points him towards the desperate needs of a people who are being oppressed.

When considering questions of purpose or calling, the modern Western tendency is often to begin with the self. We try to discover our purpose through an investigation into ourselves. We start by thinking about what we are good at, what we enjoy, what we are passionate about, and then from this self-knowledge we try to work out what we should be doing with our lives.

---

* Mark 1:11; Matthew 4:3, 6, 9; Luke 4:3, 7, 9.

There are elements of this approach which can be helpful, but simply looking within is not enough to discern the call that God has on our lives. For it is often our context which drives our actions and draws out our purpose. We are not simply to look for a suitable context for our characters. For example, Jesus' famous 'Parable of the Good Samaritan'* is not the story of someone passionate about helping Jewish men who had been the victims of injustice, giving the man he comes across assistance because this might be a good fit for his skills and experience. He simply helps the one he comes across. Martin Luther King Jr didn't look around for a good cause to fit his skillset before finally deciding that civil rights in America could work well for him. He didn't spend his early life thinking that he would love to organize boycotts, go on marches, give stirring speeches and hopefully win a Nobel Peace Prize. Instead, he found himself in a context which was deeply unjust, and this drew out of him the great purpose of his life.

One of the main driving forces for the ministry of Jesus was his compassion, which was his love for those around him who were hurting and who were far from God. The works he performed, which revealed his divinity and established God's kingdom on earth, were usually a response to the context he found himself in, healing the sick who were brought to him, releasing the oppressed who were shouting at him and multiplying food for the hungry crowds surrounding him. Sometimes the key question is not so much what we want to do, or what we would be good at doing, but simply what needs to be done around us. God wants us to see what is around us and respond with compassion.

FACING THE PAST

God's call often requires us to face pain we have experienced and the mistakes we have made. Moses was in the desert because he was running away from his past. There was the pain of knowing that

* Luke 10:25–37.

he was an Israelite, brutally oppressed by a dominant nation. Then he had made a serious mistake, killing an Egyptian to protect an Israelite who was being beaten by his slavedriver, before escaping to Midian to avoid punishment when it had been discovered. He had tried to make things better but had ended up making things worse.

Egypt was the place where his own people had been enslaved and murdered, and where he had got it so badly wrong. It was not a place where he was welcome. It is understandable that he was reluctant to return to Egypt, to the place of failure, and where he had been hurt and rejected. But often God's call on our lives means having to face our past and return to the place of failure.

When I think through my life, I can think of so many mistakes, so many failures, so many regrets. And there are also times where I have been hurt by others. These experiences cause pain, and our natural inclination is to avoid pain, therefore we run from our past hurts, our past mistakes. But God's call means being willing to face the past, the ways we've been hurt or have hurt other people. We all have a past, but it need not be an obstacle to our future if we are willing to face it instead of avoiding it.

When, in June 2021, I first suggested to Tara that we think about Brazil again, her first response was, 'I think that chapter is closed.' She had felt called there when she was a teenager, but it had never quite happened. Then, while we were dating, she had gone on a three-week mission trip to volunteer in a project working with children in the interior of Brazil, but she had not enjoyed it. She didn't connect with Brazil as a place, nor did the work spark anything within her. She left feeling confused, wondering what that sense of calling over all those years had been about, and assuming that she would only find out in heaven. For her that part of her life was over.

So, when I brought up the possibility of going to Brazil, Tara was initially reluctant to open that door again. But she did open it, facing the confusion and disappointment of the past, and in doing so opened herself up to the calling which God had for us.

WORKING IN WEAKNESS

As we meet with God, he calls us to work in weakness. On some levels God's calling of Moses to go to Egypt and speak to Pharaoh about the Hebrew people makes sense. Moses grew up in Pharaoh's court in Egypt. He knew the language of both the Egyptians and the Hebrews. He knew Egyptian customs and culture and the way the court worked. He was also now experienced in working in the desert, having been a shepherd there, and so would be able to lead the Israelites through this land, knowing the sources of water and food along the way.

Moses would be operating in some of his strengths. But going to Egypt would also mean working in weakness too. Moses struggled with his speech and God was asking him to undertake what was primarily a speaking role. He had been discredited as a leader with both the Egyptians and the Hebrews. In calling Moses to go back to Egypt, the land he had fled from, and speak to Pharaoh on behalf of the people who had rejected him, God was calling Moses to work in weakness.

It is striking that God waits until this moment to call Moses. I might have thought that Moses was best placed to liberate the Israelites before his great failure and flight to Midian, when he was in Pharoah's court, powerful, influential, well-connected and respected, an insider who could work from within to improve the prospects of the Israelites. But God waits until he has failed, when he is disgraced, hated and in exile. He waits until Moses is an outsider and then calls him back to Egypt. He waits until he is weak, and then calls him.

In coming to pastor Christ Church in Rio I was conscious of two things in particular which I had been keen to avoid for as long as possible: conflict and responsibility. I'm overly sensitive and easily fall apart in the presence of conflict, so I prefer to operate in environments where everyone likes one another (and, if possible, me) and gets on well. And I try to avoid responsibility, preferring it if someone else is the one ultimately in charge. Being an associate pastor in Brighton was the ideal role for me, because all the unpopular decisions tended to be focused on the senior pastor. I used to tell people jokingly that I just wanted 'power without responsibility'! Given the choice, I would always choose no influence and no responsibility, over influence and responsibility.

But coming to Rio meant that I would have to operate in both these weaknesses: I would have to take responsibility and I would have to face conflict – more than I had anticipated – and even hostility, which surprised and threw me. So much within me would want to run away in those first few months.

We do not discover the purpose of our lives by simply trying to find the best fit for our strengths, skills and experience. For God's call often takes place at the intersection of our strengths and weaknesses. He uses both, calling us to work in our strengths, but also in our weaknesses.

USING WHAT WE HAVE

As we meet with God, he asks us to focus on what we have, instead of worrying about what we lack. As God continues to persuade Moses to accept his calling, he asks him, 'What is that in your hand?' (4:2). He asks him to recognize what he already has. He has something very ordinary, his staff, which represents his skill, his profession. God transforms it into a snake and then back into a staff. It was to be a sign to the Egyptians of God's presence with him. God takes an object which was used for ordinary purposes, transforming it into something which could be used for extraordinary purposes. God is always willing to take the ordinary things which we have in our hands and do extraordinary things through them.

We can limit ourselves by focusing on what we lack. We think to ourselves, 'I would start running every day if only I had some proper running shoes. I would be more generous if only I had more money. I would be more hospitable if only I was married. I would be able to help other people if only I had more time. I would be able to serve the poorest in Rio if only I spoke better Portuguese.'

But God asks us, 'What do you already have?' Instead of wishing we had more, or waiting till we have more, we can give him what we have now and see what he does with it. For this staff, which would have felt so ordinary, was the same staff which was used to bring plagues upon Egypt, divide the Red Sea, and bring water from a rock. The ordinary becomes extraordinary when it is given to God.

STARTING SMALL

The story that God invites us to be a part of can start small. This life-changing encounter started for Moses with a little curiosity to see why a bush was on fire but not burning up. Then Moses responds obediently to God's first command, which is to take off his sandals, an easy request, especially when compared with what would follow. When Moses eventually agrees to go to Egypt he does not say to his father-in-law, 'I'm going down to Egypt to confront the most powerful man in the world, liberate his slaves and lead them across the desert to bring them, against all odds, to their own land, thereby establishing a new nation, which will play an essential part in God's purposes for humanity, eventually leading to God's own entry into, and salvation of, the whole world.' Instead, he says to Jethro, 'Let me return to my own people in Egypt *to see if any of them are still alive*' (4:18). His confidence and ambitions are so small at this stage. He is not returning to Egypt to liberate his people, to defeat the Egyptians or to enact a story that will define a people for thousands of years. He is simply going to see if there's anyone alive. This is how our purpose with God often starts: with a first, tiny step. We agree to have a conversation, or to start praying about something, or visit a country the other side of the world just to see, but it is only the start of God's extraordinary plans.

When I first felt called to ordination in the Church of England, I was not at all happy with the idea of becoming a vicar or church leader. I looked with dread at the whole process of selection and training, and certainly didn't want to end up pastoring a church somewhere. But something was stirring in me, and the first step was to talk to my own vicar about calling. That happened to be my father, and I thought I could probably do that. When I'd had that conversation, I had to speak to another pastor at the church, which I was happy to do. Then there was a form to fill in, and by that time I felt I could manage that. And so things progressed, step by step, and at each stage I was only willing to do the next thing, but eventually God brought me to where he was wanting me to go.

God, in his infinite kindness and patience, allows us to start small, taking each obedient step, which he lays out in front of us, drawing us slowly into his purposes.

REALIZING IT IS NOT ABOUT US

Most importantly, as we meet with God, we realize that our lives are not centred on ourselves. In this story Moses struggles to accept the call of God, because he remains fixated on himself, what he wants, what he is good at and how it will work out for him. But this story is not the story of Moses, it is the story of God and his purpose to rescue the people of Israel. The book of Exodus does not begin with the birth of Moses, but with a people who need to be rescued and a God who is full of compassion for them and has a purpose for them. If we try to get God to fit into our story it will always be too small. If we are willing to fit into God's story, then we get to be part of something extraordinary.

This story is about God's identity more than our identity. God calls out, 'Moses, Moses', reminding Moses of his identity, but much more significant than the reminder of Moses' name is the revelation to Moses of God's name, Yahweh, and his identity as 'I AM WHO I AM' (3:14). He is the one who is not defined by anyone else, nor limited by anyone or anything. If we make our purpose about ourselves, it is necessarily limited. If we make our lives about God's purpose, then we are connected to something unlimited.

It is about God's compassion, more than our passions. Moses should have been passionate about rescuing his enslaved fellow Israelites, who included members of his own family. His brother Aaron was there, and his sister Miriam. His nephews were there, and probably many other cousins and nieces and uncles and aunts. But he doesn't seem to be passionate about this cause. The question, 'What is your passion?' might be helpful to some degree, but it is not enough for our purpose to emerge. Much more important is what God is passionate about. Our passions are far too small, but God's compassion is vast. Our passions go up and down; God's compassion remains constant.

And it's about God's presence, more than our abilities. Moses' response to God's repeated promises of his presence is almost comical. God reassures Moses by saying, 'I will be with you' (3:12) – it is God who will do the work. God, not Moses, is the one who will rescue the Israelites and bring them into the Promised Land. And yet Moses seems to doubt whether God's presence will really help in the circumstances.

For much of my adult life Cristiano Ronaldo and Lionel Messi were the greatest footballers in the world. If one day Ronaldo and Messi (in their prime) and I (also in my prime) decided to go to the park for an informal game of football and were challenged to a game of three on three by some people playing there, I should be confident of victory (even in Brazil). If my new friends Messi and Ronaldo looked at me and said, 'We can win this', it would be strange if I responded by saying, 'I don't think we can. I haven't got my proper football boots on and I'm a bit weak on my left foot. And my acceleration is not great. Knowing my own weaknesses, I just don't think we can beat them.' They would then say, 'But we are with you. We are going to win.' And if I said, 'Yes, that's great, but my passing isn't as accurate as it could be and I'm a bit rusty in goal, so we will probably lose,' they would rightly conclude that I was totally self-obsessed, and I should look again to see who is with me. God tells Moses that he will be with him. He tells him that he will do it. This is enough.

ALWAYS UNFINISHED

Accepting the story which God has for us will mean that our purpose will always be unfinished. For it is not really our purpose but God's purpose being worked through us. If we make our purpose about ourselves, we might complete it. We might aim to become Prime Minister or President and achieve this goal, or we could try to become a millionaire and be successful. But if our purpose is about ending poverty, creating equality, bringing justice or making disciples of all nations, our purpose will always be unfulfilled. Moses would die before his task was completed. He would not get to the Promised Land. Winston Churchill would never see a free Europe, Martin Luther King Jr didn't get to see racial equality in America, slavery still exists today, long after the deaths of those who campaigned for the end of the institution in the nineteenth century. Great callings always remain unfinished.

There is only one who ever gets to say, 'It is finished.'* Jesus Christ is the one with the great purpose. He is the one who embraced disruption and came from heaven to earth to live a human life. He is the one who worked in weakness, taking on human flesh in all its weakness. He is the one who faced the past; not his own, but the past of humanity, with all its pain and mistakes. He faced the past of the Israelites who failed in the desert before they reached the Promised Land, going into another desert and resisting temptation.

* John 19:30.

He faced the past of humanity, for Adam and Eve had insisted on their will against God's in the Garden of Eden, but Jesus would go into another garden and pray, 'not my will, but yours be done.'* He is the one who knew exactly who he was, who connected to his context and, moved with compassion, loved all those he came across. When he was asked what was in his hands, the answer was the two nails holding him to a cross, made of ordinary wood, like a staff. In the hands of Jesus, this had become the means of salvation for the world.

He is the centre of history, the main character in the story of humanity, the one it has all been about. It is his story, his purpose. And we are simply given the opportunity to join in with his great purpose.

Here at the beginning of Exodus, Moses is so self-obsessed that he resists joining in with God's purpose to rescue his people. But later in the story, when Israel fails God so seriously by making a golden calf and worshipping it instead of God, God offers Moses the chance to start again and make a nation out of him. God gives Moses the chance to make the story all about him, but Moses refuses, and he would be known as 'a very humble man, more humble than anyone else on the face of the earth.'** And the one who at the burning bush couldn't grasp that God was with him, would later be the one whom God would talk with 'face to face, as one speaks to a friend.'*** He would know the presence of God more closely and intimately than anyone until the coming of Jesus.

Each of us will face a moment in our lives when we have the chance to make it all about ourselves. But our purpose is not about us. Our calling is to attach ourselves to the one with the great purpose, the one who is called, the one that the story of the world is all about.

* Luke 22:42.
** Numbers 14:2–19; 12:3.
*** Exodus 33:11.

Chapter 6

STEPPING UP AND STEPPING OUT

Joshua
Joshua 1

Be strong and very courageous. Be careful to obey all the law my servant Moses gave you; do not turn from it to the right or to the left, that you may be successful wherever you go. Keep this Book of the Law always on your lips; meditate on it day and night, so that you may be careful to do everything written in it. Then you will be prosperous and successful. Have I not commanded you? Be strong and courageous. Do not be afraid; do not be discouraged, for the LORD your God will be with you wherever you go.

JOSHUA 1:7–9

When God finds a person determined to obey him, then he takes the life of that person in his hands, like the helm of a boat or the reins of a horse.

RANIERO CANTALAMESSA*

Sometimes the call of God means embarking on something which feels totally new. Abraham is called to leave Ur and go to a new land, Joseph to create and implement a new feeding project for the people

---

* Raniero Cantalamessa, *Obedience*, tr. Frances Lonergan Villa (St Paul Publications, 1989), p55.

of Egypt, and Moses to start a liberation project for the people of Israel. In similar ways God calls individuals and groups to what is new: to start a business, to plant a church, to establish a charity or social enterprise. Or we might be called to begin a new relationship, or to 'start a family' by bringing children into the world.

However, very often we are called, not to start something new, but to continue with a work which has already begun. This was the case for Joshua. He had been working as Moses' assistant for four decades, helping Moses with the great project of liberating the Hebrew slaves from Egypt, leading them through the desert, helping them to receive God's instructions through the Law and bringing them into the Promised Land. And now, with Moses dead, God calls Joshua to continue the work which Moses had started, commanding him to bring the Israelites into the land which had been promised to their ancestors. This is the call to carry on, to play our part in something which existed before our involvement and will probably exist after our involvement ends. This is the calling we receive when we work in a business, a hospital, a school or a church, where the work has begun and God is prompting us to continue that work.

The fact that it is a continuation, rather than a whole new enterprise, does not make it any easier. To accept this calling, Joshua would have to step up. Up until now he has been Moses' assistant. He has gone with Moses wherever Moses has gone or done for Moses whatever Moses has asked him to do. He went up Mount Sinai with Moses to help with the receiving of the Ten Commandments; he fought battles whilst Moses prayed with Aaron and Hur; he went on the mission to spy out the land which Moses had organized.* When he has spoken, it has been to Moses, not to the people. When he and Caleb and the other spies returned from their mission to find out about Canaan, it is Caleb who speaks up, with Joshua supporting him.** It seems like Joshua preferred to take a secondary

* Exodus 24:12–13; 17:10; Numbers 13:16.
** Numbers 13:30; 14:6–9.

role, supporting, helping and encouraging, but letting others take the lead.

But now God was calling him to step up and lead the Israelites. He would have to speak to the Israelites. He would need to embrace a new way of working, significantly different from how he had worked before. And whereas before, when the Israelites had complained and grumbled (as they had done frequently over the past forty years) it has been against Moses; now Joshua should expect to receive the complaints himself.

Perhaps it comes from growing up with an older brother, whom I followed around for most of my childhood (and the first part of my adult life), but I've always preferred the role of assistant. I almost never want to take the lead, but like helping, advising and encouraging those in the lead. Playing sport, I would never want to be captain, but I would like to be close to the captain, giving my suggestions of what I thought they should be doing. And I certainly never wanted to become a senior pastor, or vicar. In Brighton I had what seemed to me the ideal role of associate vicar. I loved it. I could offer my advice, help influence what happened, do whatever I could to help Archie and Sam Coates, who were leading the church, but I was not the one who was ultimately responsible. If anything went wrong, or if anyone was unhappy, I was not normally the one to get the blame.

But it seems like just when we are comfortable operating in one way, God calls us to step into a new way of living, working and relating to other people. One of the most frightening aspects of moving to Rio was the realization that I would have to be the senior pastor. I would have to take responsibility. I would need to lead. It would require me to step up.

Stepping up for Joshua would mean facing challenges which many of us naturally avoid. Commentators sometimes point out that the first half of the book of Joshua is uncomfortably violent, with lots of battles and killing, and the second half of the book is quite boring, with lots of lists of people and places, as Joshua divides up the land for the Israelites. This fits my experience of responding to God's call: it involves more conflict (though no killing, yet!) than you were hoping for, and a lot more administration than you were expecting. You face opposition and discover people hating you and attacking you, and you also need to fill in a lot of forms, apply for visas, reply to emails, make lists and try to be organized.

Responding to God's call means stepping up; it also means stepping out. And stepping out into the unknown. God was calling the Israelites to cross the Jordan and enter a land they did not know. Only Joshua and Caleb had ever been there, and that was only a brief tour forty years before. Otherwise, this was a step into the unknown for God's people. There would be new enemies, new challenges, new opportunities. They couldn't stay where they were, they had to step out and move forward.

It is a call to step out despite significant obstacles. For Joshua, there was the river Jordan in front of them, and then the impressive walls of Jericho not far away, and no obvious way through them. He faced a natural obstacle (a river) and an obstacle created by other people (huge walls), and at this point Joshua has no solution for either of them. When God calls us to step out, it is often despite many obstacles – financial, practical and logistical – which, at the point at which he calls us, apparently have no solution.

It is a call to step out despite the hostile forces confronting us. Across the Jordan were several nations who wanted to kill Joshua and the people he was leading. So he was stepping out into a place filled with enemies. For us too, when we step out, we inevitably step out into opposition, criticism and hostility. Ultimately, we are stepping out into a spiritual battle, not fighting 'flesh and blood', but against plenty of 'spiritual forces of evil' which are opposed to us.*

Finally, it is a call to step out despite the failures of the past. Joshua and the Israelites had been in this position before. Forty years previously, Joshua and Caleb and the other spies had gone into

---

* Ephesians 6:12.

Canaan, returning with a report that the land was good, but that the people who lived there were strong, the cities fortified and that they were weak in comparison to the Canaanites. Caleb and Joshua had tried to persuade the people that they could do it, but unsuccessfully. The people had lost their nerve, refusing to enter the land, and so God told them they would have to wait for another forty years. In response, the people foolishly decided they would try to enter the land after all, but against God's will and without his presence, and they had been routed.* The whole episode had been a terrible failure. Caleb and Joshua had failed to persuade the people, and the people had failed to believe God's promises or follow his commands.

Now God was calling Joshua to step out again, to persuade the Israelites to do what they had failed to do all those years ago, to get right what they had previously got wrong and to change patterns of behaviour which had been so disastrous for them before.

For all these reasons, stepping up and stepping out can feel terrifying. We can find ourselves holding back instead of stepping out. We might want to step down more than step up. Perhaps this is how Joshua felt. Maybe this is how you feel. But God tells us how we can fulfil the calling he has for us. For he commands Joshua,

> *Be strong and very courageous. Be careful to obey all the law my servant Moses gave you; do not turn from it to the right or to the left, that you may be successful wherever you go. Keep this Book of the Law always on your lips; meditate on it day and night, so that you may be careful to do everything written in it. Then you will be prosperous and successful.*
>
> JOSHUA 1:7-8

There is one simple way for Joshua to do what he is called to do, and become the person he is called to be, to fulfil the role he is meant to fulfil: obedience. It is total obedience, courageous obedience and it is effective obedience.

---

* Numbers 13 – 14.

TOTAL OBEDIENCE

When God commands Joshua to enter the land, he does so by commanding total obedience. He tells Joshua to be careful to obey *all* the law. It is not enough to be obedient in some ways or at some times. He insists he obeys 'carefully' (1:7), for we are not to assume we know what God will say or what we should do. Later, the Israelites would be deceived by the Gibeonites, because 'they did not enquire of the LORD' (9:14). They were overconfident and careless, thinking they could work out what to do without stopping to ask God for his wisdom and guidance. And he warns them against *distraction*, against turning aside 'to the right or to the left' (1:7), which is where we get diverted and go off course, through a career, a lifestyle or a relationship which leads us away from our relationship with God.

Total obedience will mean listening to God's voice carefully and continually (1:8), always thinking about God's Word ('meditate on it'), speaking God's Word ('always on your lips') and doing God's Word ('to do everything written in it'). It is the command to make sure that God's voice is the first, the most frequent and the most powerful voice in our lives. Forty years earlier they had failed because God's voice had been drowned out by the voices of fear and doubt. Now Joshua needed to make sure that God's voice would be stronger than any other. This is the pathway to knowing and fulfilling God's call on our lives.

There seem to be three main ways we can approach the idea of calling or purpose. The first is to start with the self. We try to understand ourselves, who we are, our characters and personalities, our passions and desires, and then attempt to fit our life's purpose around these things. This is the pursuit of authenticity, the desire to be truly ourselves, in our work, our relationships, in the way that we live our lives.

There is something good in this approach, for when God calls us, he does so by revealing who we are, reminding us of who we are and transforming who we are. But we need something more than the self to work out the direction of our lives. For one thing, it is not always clear to us who we *really* are, which of our skills and gifts we should be using or how to resolve the conflict between our competing desires. But more importantly, there is a danger that we will try to fit the world around our self, seemingly in pursuit of authenticity, but in the end become self-centred.

The second approach is to start with others. The course of our lives is shaped by those around us, the needs of friends and family, of our local community or our nation. We do what needs to be done, based on the context in which we find ourselves, the nature of the community around us and the problems we see in the world. This is the pursuit of service, or doing our duty, the desire to 'make a difference' or 'to make the world a better place'.

Again, there is much that is valuable in this approach, for when God calls us, he does so by connecting us to our contexts, prompting us to respond to the needs around us, getting us to look outwards to a world which is broken and hurting. But we need something more than just those around us to work out our calling. For the needs which surround us are endless, and we can become overwhelmed, trying to work out what exactly we should be doing in response to the infinite problems we see around us. Sometimes our efforts to make a difference end up making things worse. There is a danger that we can find ourselves fitting in with what the world needs of us, becoming so consumed with trying to help everyone that we lose ourselves in the process.

But there is a third approach, to start not with the self or with others, but with God himself. This is the life of obedience. Authenticity is alignment to our true selves, service is the alignment of our lives to the needs of others, but obedience is alignment to the will of God. Instead of starting by listening to the self or to others, we begin by listening to God, to the one who loves us perfectly, who understands us completely, who alone has perfect plans for serving and saving a broken and hurting world. Instead of seeking authenticity or service, we seek obedience.

Obedience means listening carefully to God, seeking to do his will and following his paths. As we seek to follow God's call on our lives, there will be times when it feels like our desires and God's desires overlap. We felt this when we went to Brighton in 2009. We loved Brighton, we could see it was a good fit for us and it made a lot of sense. There are other times when following God's call overlaps with our desire to serve others and make a difference. When we felt called to start a night shelter for rough sleepers in Brighton, it wasn't an obviously good fit for my skills, but I could see how it would make a difference by getting homeless men and women off the streets through the coldest months of the year. There may even be times when being obedient to God feels like it is a great fit with our characters and with our desire to make a difference, making the choice to follow God's call relatively easy.

However, there will also be occasions when following God's call on our lives means simply being obedient. For example, our arrival in Rio de Janeiro did not emerge out of an attempt to be authentic, for so much of what would be required of us here did not feel like a good fit for us; and it certainly wasn't the result of looking around for where we could be most helpful. It felt like a call from God to be obedient, no matter where it took us or what it meant.

Being a Christian requires more than asking God's help to be authentic and to serve those around us; it requires us to make a decision to be obedient to him in all things. The Christian life demands more than trying to have a balance between the self, the needs of others and God, keeping the competing requirements of each in tension – becoming a Christian means placing ourselves completely in the hands of God and choosing to obey him in all things. To follow Jesus is to place ourselves completely in the circle of obedience.

However, as we do this, we begin to discover that obedience to God leads to the authenticity which we have always longed for and enables us to serve the world more effectively and powerfully than we could ever have imagined. As we pursue obedience, God's will for us, our authenticity and our desire to make a difference begin to overlap more and more.

Jesus was and is the most authentic human being to have lived, the only person in the history of the world who was truly himself, the only person who could proclaim simply and without qualification, 'I am'.* He is also the Saviour of the world, who alone has served the world perfectly. And he is these things because he is primarily the obedient Son of the Father, doing what his heavenly Father asks of him. If you want to be authentic, be obedient. If you want to change the world, be obedient.

George Müller was born in 1805, in what then was Prussia, becoming a Christian in 1825. However, at first he was not quite ready to give himself totally to God, wanting to hold on to parts of his old life. But then came a breakthrough in 1829: 'I gave myself fully to the Lord. Honour, pleasure, money, my physical powers, my mental powers, all was laid down at the feet of Jesus, and I became a great lover of the Word of God. I found my all in God.'**

He moved to England, got married and became a pastor. Soon after he decided to give up his salary, trusting in God to provide for their needs instead. Moreover, he and his wife resolved that they would never ask anyone to help them financially in any way.

Then, at a time when the streets of Bristol were filled with children, they felt called to start an orphanage, operating with the same fundraising principles which they had for themselves personally. Müller wanted to live in such a way that the reality of God and his miraculous provision would be evident to everyone. And it was, for God provided for him, for the orphan houses and for the salaries of those who worked there. This approach to his finances was not a stressful one for Müller. Rather, it appeared to others that he was without a care in the world. And the

* John 8:58.
** Roger Steer, *George Müller: Delighted in God* (Christian Focus, 1997), p26.

impact he had through these houses was immense.

When he died in 1898, the whole city of Bristol mourned. On the day of his funeral businesses and shops closed, and thousands lined the streets for the procession. One newspaper wrote of him that 'Müller had robbed the cruel streets of thousands of victims, the gaols of thousands of felons, the workhouse of thousands of helpless waifs.' Another wrote, 'Thousands of children have been fed, clothed and educated out of funds which have poured in without appeal or advertisement of any sort. How was this wonder accomplished? Mr Müller told the world that it was the result of "Prayer".'*

Müller lived a joyful and impactful life. And he was able to do this because it was primarily an obedient life.

COURAGEOUS OBEDIENCE

God calls us to total obedience, and this requires courage from us. God commands Joshua, 'Be strong and very courageous' (1:7), for living obediently is impossible without courage. The obedient option is almost always the courageous option. Courage alone is insufficient. Forty years earlier the Israelites eventually found their courage and attempted to invade the Promised Land, but it was not obedient courage and so they were defeated. History has many examples of courage which has not been obedient to God and caused great suffering. We are called to courage *and* obedience: to courageous obedience and obedient courage.

Courageous obedience sometimes involves standing strong despite pressures, internal and external. In our first two years in Brazil, I found myself thinking frequently of the film *Chariots of Fire*, which tells the true story of Eric Liddell, the missionary and athlete. Liddell was part of the British Olympic team which was due to compete in the 1924 Olympics in Paris, but he refused to run in the heats for the 100m sprints because they took place on a

* ibid, pp231–232.

Sunday. He wanted to run. There was intense pressure to run, from his friends, his team and the British Olympic committee, as people tried to persuade him to place his loyalty to his country and to the team ahead of his loyalty to God. But he would not be moved. And yet God provided a way, and he was able to fulfil his calling to run (and win) and to be a missionary in China.

At other times courageous obedience involves us stepping out when no one else does. In November 1882 the great evangelist DL Moody accepted an invitation to do an eight-day mission at Cambridge University. He had already had a significant impact in the United Kingdom and in the USA, preaching to millions of people, changing lives and society in those nations. But Cambridge University was considered one of the most intolerant and hostile audiences in the world, with its 3500 undergraduates from privileged and wealthy backgrounds. Moody had left school aged thirteen and said that he had never had more anxiety than when he approached Cambridge University to preach there.

On the first day of the mission the students mocked his American accent, bursting into laughter when he spoke. Whenever he pronounced the word, 'Daniel' as 'Dan'l', they would all shout back 'Dan'l, Dan'l'. One, a student named Gerald Lander, said of him, 'If uneducated men *will* come to teach the Varsity they deserve to be snubbed.'*

After this inauspicious start to the mission, Moody was reluctant to continue the mission. But the following day, Lander, who had been the ringleader of those mocking him, was persuaded to go and apologize to Moody. Moody met with him and agreed to preach again, but told him that proof of his apology would be if he appeared at the next meeting.

The Wednesday meeting came, in the same gymnasium, but it was now fuller. Moody preached again. He ended by asking anyone

* E Michael Rusten & Sharon O Rusten, *The One Year Christian History* (Tyndale House, 2003).

who wanted to know Christ to go up to the fencing gallery by ascending an iron staircase in the centre of the hall, in full view of everyone. In a context where students hated showing emotions, or appearing undignified, this was a strong disincentive to respond.

No one moved. Moody asked a second time. Nobody moved. He asked a third time. Again, nobody moved. The fourth time he asked, a young man left his place at the back, half hid his face in his gown, and practically ran up the staircase two steps at a time, with the noise ringing out across the room: 'Clang, clang, clang.' Another followed, and then another. Soon the whole room was filled with the clanging of feet as man after man went up to the gallery.

We do not know the name of that first man to respond that day. But we do the names of some of the 51 others. One of them was Gerald Lander, who became a missionary bishop in South China. Hundreds of students decided to follow Jesus that week, including some of the most influential Christians of the early twentieth century. It is considered one of the most significant weeks in the history of Christianity. But I often think of that first man to move, the one whose name is not remembered, but who had the courage to step out first.

EFFECTIVE OBEDIENCE

This obedience is an effective obedience, for it is the method by which Joshua will lead the people into Canaan and take hold of the land. It is through obedience that Joshua will be 'prosperous and successful' (1:8). Joshua will have to navigate all kinds of difficult problems and work out the right strategy for each of them, and it is through obedience that he is successful.

One of the striking features of the conquest of the land is that, with each challenge and each battle, Joshua knows what he should do in that situation. He doesn't assume that what worked in one place will work in another. It would have been understandable if, after the success of conquering Jericho, Joshua had determined to use the same tactic of marching around every city until their walls also fell down. But Joshua knows that each battle – Jericho, Ai, the five kings of the Amorites – requires different tactics and different miracles. And for each he needs to hear God's voice, and through being obedient to God's direction, Joshua is able to win every battle.

It seems that Joshua's ability to hear God's voice for each situation emerges from his habit of reading the Law and meditating on it day and night. The frequent habit of spending time with God's revealed Word enables Joshua to get to know God's voice so well that, when he is facing the difficult decisions which come his way, he knows what God is directing him to do.

The regular habit of reading the Bible is essential for Christians, because it enables us to get to know God, to learn to recognize his voice, to live in relationship with him and to live in accordance with his will for our lives. It is also essential for when we are looking for guidance on which direction we should take and for strategies in complicated situations, even when the answers are not found directly in the Bible. For as we read the Bible, we become more familiar with God's voice, which makes it easier to discern God's promptings about which way to go when the answers are not obvious. If you want to know God's specific will for your life, start by getting to know God's general will for your life, which we discover through reading the Bible. Joshua will study God's Word, and this will help him to discern God's voice as God directs his steps.

Joshua and the people of God have been in the desert for many years. They have heard God's voice and recorded his Law. But the danger is that as soon as they enter the land, everything they have learnt and been told will get lost. At this point God's will may have seemed clear, but after they are in the land it may have felt less so.

In *The Silver Chair*, by CS Lewis, Aslan gives Jill certain instructions or 'signs' which are essential for her to fulfil her purpose in Narnia. He says to her,

But, first, remember, remember, remember the signs. Say them to yourself when you wake in the morning and when you lie down at night, and when you wake in the middle of the night. And whatever strange things may happen to you, let nothing turn your mind from following the signs ... And the signs which you have learned here will not look at all as you expect them to look, when you meet them there. That is why it is so important to know them by heart and pay no attention to appearances. Remember the signs and believe the signs. Nothing else matters.*

LOVING OBEDIENCE

This obedience, which is essential to the Christian life, and which is foundational to us fulfilling our calling, is a loving obedience. Before he commands obedience, God reminds Joshua of his promises: to give him good things, to be with him, to grant him success (1:3–5). We obey God because we are loved by God. We seek to do God's will because he has rescued us.

But we will always fail to be obedient. We can never obey God fully or completely. Even at our best we are half-hearted, and partial, and distracted in our obedience. We always fail to be totally obedient or courageously obedient. This is why thousands of years later another Joshua (which in Greek is 'Jesus') would come into this same land which Joshua entered. He would step out from heaven and face not just physical obstacles and military obstacles, but the great spiritual obstacles of sin and shame and death itself. He would face not just the failures of one generation of Israelites but the failures of every generation of all nations. His obedience would be total, courageous and born of total love for his Father. And 'through the obedience of the one man the many will be made righteous.'**

---

* CS Lewis, *The Silver Chair* (HarperCollins, 2014), p37.
** Romans 5:19.

Chapter 7

BUILDING UP AND STRIPPING BACK

Gideon
Judges 6 – 7

When the angel of the LORD appeared to Gideon, he said, 'The LORD is with you, mighty warrior.'

JUDGES 6:12

'Pardon me, my lord,' Gideon replied, 'but how can I save Israel? My clan is the weakest in Manasseh, and I am the least in my family.'

JUDGES 6:15

You come from nothing. You're nothing. But not to me.

STAR WARS: THE LAST JEDI*

On 21 August 2015 Anthony Sadler, Alek Skarlatos and Spencer Stone boarded the crowded 15:17 train from Amsterdam to Paris. They had been best friends at high school in America and had been on a trip travelling through Europe.

When the train stopped in Brussels, Ayoub El Khazzani, an ISIS operative, got on the front of the train carrying an AK-47, a handgun and enough ammunition to kill everyone on board. Anthony, Alek and Spencer were sitting near the front of the train, listening to music and

---

* Rian Johnson, *Star Wars: The Last Jedi* (Walt Disney Studios Motion Pictures, 2017).

sending messages, when they saw a man in a suit sprint down the aisle past them. They turned to see a man with his shirt off, holding a gun, and instinctively they got up from their seats and ran towards him.

The man took aim at them, but the gun didn't go off. Spencer hit him, and the four of them fought furiously until eventually Spencer got him into a Jujitsu hold which caused him to pass out. They tied him up, and then Spencer noticed a passenger bleeding heavily from the neck. He put his fingers into the man's neck and stopped the bleeding, saving his life.

Initial reports claimed that a terrorist attack had been thwarted by three marines, but this wasn't true. Anthony was a student. Alek had been on tour in Afghanistan but was effectively working as security whilst the special forces went on their various missions. Spencer had tried to get into the Airforce pararescue but had failed. He had then applied for 'SERE', preparing people for being caught behind enemy lines, but had failed again. He had started working as a janitor and was training as an emergency medical technician.

They were three ordinary people, but they had done something extraordinary, saving the lives of 554 passengers. They were phoned the next day by the American President Barack Obama, and later received the highest order of merit in France, the Legion of Honour.

God's call on our lives often leads to extraordinary things taking place: the birth of a nation, the liberation of slaves, the defeat of oppressors, the rebuilding of a city, the start of a dynasty, the entrance of God into the world, the planting of churches around the Mediterranean. However, God does not choose extraordinary people. Esther may have been beautiful, Moses had been an Egyptian prince, and Paul was clearly intelligent and well-educated, but mostly those who are called are not exceptional. These stories of calling are about ordinary people, called to play their parts in the extraordinary purposes of God.

The standard pattern for a superhero story seems to be that an individual discovers they are exceptionally strong, fast, rich, clever or good at flying, and then after discovering their abilities they realize that they have a purpose to help people, defeat villains and save the world. However, the stories of calling in the Bible start with God calling ordinary people who end up doing extraordinary things. They are not called because they are extraordinary; they become extraordinary because they are called.

This is what we find in the story of Gideon, an ordinary Israelite, hiding from the enemy and simply trying to survive. He does not think he is better than everyone else. If anything, he recognizes that he is less than others. But this ordinary man will receive God's calling and free his people from oppression, defeating the Midianites who are far stronger and more numerous than the Israelites.

The angel greets Gideon with the words: 'The LORD is with you, mighty warrior' (6:12). This is a strange way for God to speak to him because Gideon is quite clearly not a mighty warrior. He has not defeated an army of Midianites. He is threshing wheat in a winepress because he is hiding from the Midianites. He is afraid, and he's not an important person. In fact, he says that he is the least in his family (6:15).

I know how he feels. I was also the least in my family growing up. I have an elder brother and a younger sister, both of whom are extraordinary people. In our mid-twenties they both trained as lawyers, moved to Bangalore in India, and worked for justice organizations rescuing people from slavery. Whereas I trained to be a vicar, joined the Church of England, and moved to Brighton to live by the sea. As my friend Josh once said to me, 'Becs is clearly amazing, and Henry is extraordinary. It's not that you're boring, Jonny, you're just ...' but no other adjective came to mind!

But God takes ordinary people and does something extraordinary in us and through us, building us up, getting us started, confirming our calling with signs, whilst at the same time stripping us back to enable us to do what he has called us to do.

BUILDING IDENTITY

God builds us up through his *Word*. God calls Gideon 'mighty warrior' (6:12). God sees in him a quality which Gideon doesn't see in himself and calls it out of him. We see God doing this again and again. He looks at Moses, the disgraced shepherd hiding in the hills, and sees the liberator of Egypt. He looks at Esther – beautiful and charming but not one to cause a fuss and sees the one who will confront kings and evil royal advisers and establish new laws. He looks at Simon the fisherman, keen but unreliable, and sees Peter, the rock. He looks at Saul, the persecutor of Christians, and sees Paul the church-planter. God looks at each of us with our fears, anxieties and weaknesses, our regrets from the past and struggles in the present, and he sees who he has made us to be for the purpose he wants to fulfil through us.

But this is more than God simply seeing our potential more clearly than we do ourselves. For it is not that Gideon could be a mighty warrior, if only he gave himself a chance. Instead, it is the Word of God which creates in Gideon something which was not there before. God's words do not simply articulate an existing reality; they bring a new reality into being. God's voice makes Gideon a mighty warrior.

God's Word is powerful. God created the world through his Word and God recreates us through his Word. There will have been many words spoken over you in your life: words of discouragement, words of mockery, words of condemnation and words that have shaped your self-image and self-understanding. They may have been words from the people closest to you, the subtle words communicated by our culture or the internal words which can be harsher than any others. But there is another voice that is more powerful and more significant than any of these words. When God says you are his child, you become his child. When God says you are forgiven, you are forgiven. And when God says you are a mighty warrior, you become a mighty warrior. You discover your purpose when you begin to believe what God says about you instead of what the world says about you or even what you think of yourself.

Next, God builds us up through his *presence*. He says to him, 'The LORD is with you, mighty warrior' (6:12). Gideon becomes a mighty warrior through the voice of God spoken over him and the Spirit of God coming upon him. God is not with him because he is a mighty warrior; he is a mighty warrior because God is with him. The presence of God turns Gideon into a mighty warrior. The Lord is the Almighty God, and so the presence of the Almighty makes us mighty.

The extraordinary actions of Anthony Sadler, Alek Skarlatos and Spencer Stone on the 15:17 to Paris were not just because of *what* was in them, but because of *who* was with them. All three of them had parents praying for them throughout their trip in Europe. And it seems as if there was a guiding hand on what they were doing. Anthony got a credit card approved against all expectations. They had never planned on going to Amsterdam and it felt like they had arrived there almost by accident. When they got to Amsterdam, they had such a good time they decided they wouldn't get the train on to Paris as they had planned, for, strangely, several people had tried to dissuade them from going to Paris at all. On the night before their journey, they decided they should stay in Amsterdam and get another train on another day. However, the following morning all three of them woke up feeling like they should get that train after all. To this day they still don't know why they made that decision.

When they got on that train, initially they were sitting at the back, but the Wi-Fi wasn't working well, so they decided to try moving to the front. It worked better there so that was where they settled, perfectly placed to stop the man who planned to kill everyone on that train. When they charged at Ayoub El Khazzani, the AK-47 which was aimed at them, a gun known for its reliability, didn't fire. Spencer had only learnt Jujitsu, the self-defence techniques he used to restrain El Khazzani, because it was the only free martial arts class he could find. It was only because Spencer had failed to get into pararescue that he had trained in medical care, enabling him to save the man who had been shot in the neck. Spencer, Alek and Anthony became mighty warriors because of something beyond them. It was the prayers of their parents and the guiding hand of God. Each one of them ends the book they wrote together by thanking God. God sees in us that which we cannot see in ourselves. God is with us when we cannot see it ourselves. God makes us into people who can be part of his extraordinary plans.

BUILDING CONFIDENCE

As God builds up Gideon's identity, he also builds his confidence, sending him out and getting him started with what he has called him to do. He says to him, 'Go in the strength you have and save Israel out of Midian's hand. Am I not sending you?' (6:14). But God, in his kindness and patience, does not make Gideon face the full Midianite army immediately. He takes him through a series of steps, allowing him to start small.

Gideon starts by building an altar, worshipping God there by himself. Then God calls him to tear down the altar to Baal belonging to his father, in his hometown (6:25), before he confronts the Midianites in the valley near the hill of Moreh (7:1), removing the hostile military forces who have been oppressing his people. Through these steps, he moves from the personal (his own spiritual life) to the domestic (the spiritual life of his family) to the national (the state of his nation). He starts by leading himself, then a group of ten men, before he leads an army. God allows him to experience opposition and hostility on a smaller scale before he faces the full opposition of the Midianites. God is taking him through each step, building up his confidence and experience, preparing him for the next challenge. As CS Lewis put it, 'If you do one good deed, your reward usually is to be set to do another and harder and better one.'*

* CS Lewis, *The Horse and his Boy* (HarperCollins, 2023), p157.

Significantly, God calls Gideon to address the spiritual problem before the political one. He has to remove the spiritual idolatry before he can remove the physical army. This is something we have noticed starting out in Rio de Janeiro. There are many problems all around us, political, social, financial and practical. But there are also some spiritual battles which need to be addressed so that we can make a difference in other areas. Our first couple of years here have focused on addressing the spiritual problems, through removing idols and establishing worship, so that we can make a difference more widely.

CONFIRMING SIGNS

As we begin to respond to God's calling, God confirms that we are on the right path. God speaks to Gideon at multiple times in multiple ways. He addresses him through an angel, through some clear signs, and through the dreams of the Midianites. Thankfully, God doesn't speak just once and refuse to repeat himself. He is willing to speak, and speak again, to confirm and to reassure, giving us signs to build up our confidence in our calling.

We must be cautious about following signs, to be aware of our own capacity to see what we want to see, or to misinterpret or manipulate signs to fit our own desires. In the New Testament Jesus rebukes those who demand signs.* But here Gideon asks for a sign humbly and openly. He is asking not only for a sign, but permission to ask for a sign (6:39). And the signs he receives are not the sole basis of his actions, but confirmations of other things which he has heard from God already.

Sometimes God gives us signs to confirm the calling he gives us. When, back in 2009, I was considering whether God was calling us to St Peter's in Brighton, I was living in a flat in London. In my bedroom there were some prints hanging on the walls which had belonged to my grandmother. Growing up, wherever I had lived, I

* e.g. Matthew 12:39.

had had them in my room. They were of various scenes in Brighton, including one of a church. As I prayed about whether I should go to join Archie and Sam Coates at St Peter's Brighton, I looked up at this print and for the first time saw the tiny inscription below it, 'St Peter's Church'. This was not the sole reason for moving to Brighton, but the fact that I unknowingly had a painting of St Peter's above my bed since I was twelve was a great encouragement, and felt like a sign from God, confirming that growing sense of calling.

Our decision to move to Rio in 2022 was the result of God appearing to speak to us in lots of ways over a long period of time. There was Tara's initial sense of calling to Brazil when she was a teenager. There was an email out of the blue from someone praying in Christ Church about the future of the church. There was our son's picture of a white bench and palm trees and the word 'Come'. There were the people we met here and the sense that we would love to work with them. And then there was the opposition and the difficulties. All of this taken together seemed to confirm that this might be the right thing. There was also a moment when we heard about some of the challenges here and wondered whether this really was the right thing for us. We felt suddenly confused. Then a friend (who knew nothing of our thoughts about Brazil) sent a message late at night, saying that she was praying for us, that she sensed that we had a big decision and that 'the confusion was not from the Lord.'

To enable us to take part in his extraordinary purposes, God builds us up, speaking words over us, reassuring us of his presence, getting us started, confirming and clarifying his call on us. However, at the same time, God also strips us back, removing from us those things which get in the way of our calling.

STRIPPING BACK

Gideon manages to gather 32,000 soldiers to fight the Midianites, but God tells him these are too many (7:2). He needs a smaller army.

He must become less. For to know that he is a mighty warrior, and that God is with him, he needs to have some things stripped away.

The Christian life always seems to combine these two elements of God building us up and stripping us back. On the one hand we are being built up, becoming more aware of God's love, affirmation, pleasure and delight, that we are 'fearfully and wonderfully made,'* secure in our identity as children of God. But, on the other hand, we are also being stripped back, as God removes our false identities, our idols, our selfishness, our pride, the reputation we've built up, our need for approval and recognition. God allows some things to be taken from us so that our true purpose emerges. God removes what is unnecessary so that he can reveal what is necessary. He weakens us to empower us.

In Gideon's case the process of stripping back takes place in two phases. The first phase is moderate and understandable. The other is more extreme and confusing. This seems to be how God often works when he strips us back.

In the first phase we go through something that is tough but bearable. We can see what God is doing and why he is doing it, and we are confident we can get through it to the other side. When God tells Gideon to send away those who are afraid (7:3), it might not be ideal, but it does make some sense. Fear can spread quickly in an army, so retaining only those who are fearless has some logic to it, even if it means losing more than two thirds of his men. And he still has 10,000 in his army, which at least gives him a chance.

But then comes phase two, where we go through something much more extreme, which seems to make no sense. God tells Gideon to divide his men again, keeping only those who 'lap the water with their tongues as a dog laps' (7:5, 7). Commentators have tried to work out the reason for this distinction but struggle to explain it convincingly. The result is an army stripped back to 300 men. Overall, Gideon has lost over 99% of his army.

* Psalm 139:14.

God sometimes strips us back to a position where it feels like we have lost everything, when all our hard work appears to have been futile and we seem to have nothing left. And that's exactly the point when we are ready to fulfil our purpose. In those times it can be easy to block God out, to go into ourselves, to give up. But God is stripping us back in order that we might become mighty warriors, for God's power is made perfect in weakness.*

Franklin D Roosevelt led the USA through both the Great Depression and the Second World War. He is often considered one of the greatest presidents in US history and is the only president to have won four elections. Up until 1921, everything appeared to be going well for him. He was thirty-nine years old, had five children, and had already been a vice-presidential candidate. He seemed destined for the White House. But that summer, after a swim in a pond, he caught a chill and then developed a high fever. His legs went numb and then wouldn't move. He had contracted polio. He was devastated. He worked hard to try to recover some mobility, but he remained highly disabled, struggling emotionally as a result. From then on, almost all physical activity involved a great effort. To give a speech he would have to be wheeled on to a platform, supported by braces, on which he leaned his whole weight to avoid falling. He fell, or almost fell, about five times over twenty years of making speeches.

But out of his weakness came a new empathy, humility and resilience. The personal battles he faced prepared him for the national and international challenges of the economic depression and the Second World War. His wife, Eleanor, speaking about his illness and disability, and about whether he would have become president without them, said, 'He would certainly have been President ... but a president of a different kind.'**

* 2 Corinthians 12:9.
** Nassir Ghaemi, *A First-Rate Madness: Uncovering the Links between Leadership and Mental Illness* (Penguin, 2011), pp140–141.

God has a purpose for your life and often this will need a process of stripping back so that he can do extraordinary things through you. It is true that God provides for us when he calls us, but not normally in the way that we expect or hope. God gives us what we need, but this is almost always less than we think we need. For it is when we apparently lack the necessary resources that God intervenes with his miraculous power.

GOING IN THE STRENGTH WE HAVE

Two of the biggest obstacles to fulfilling our purpose are the victim mentality and the helpless mentality. The victim mentality blames everyone else for their problems. The helpless mentality believes that nothing can be done to change the situation. Gideon starts this story with both these mentalities, believing that all his people's problems were someone else's fault, for God had abandoned them and the Midianites were oppressing them. And he also believes that nothing can be done (6:13–15). The Midianites control their economy and their military might make it impossible to stand up to them, for they have that great technological innovation of the day: the camel.

But God breaks through Gideon's victim mentality and his helpless mentality, insisting 'The LORD is with you, mighty warrior' (6:12). Then he says to him, 'Go in the strength you have' (6:14). In other words, don't think about what you cannot do, think about what you can do. Use the resources, the time, the talents that you already have.

In the spring of 1941, during the Second World War, the Italian army was struggling to invade Greece, so Hitler sent in the Twelfth Army, occupying Greece in only a few weeks. The Nazis took control of Athens, raising a huge Swastika flag at the Acropolis so that it could be seen all over the city, symbolizing total victory for the German army and total defeat for Greece.

In response, two Greek teenagers decided that something had

to be done. They knew that they couldn't defeat the whole of the Twelfth Army on their own, but they did what they knew they could do, which was to go to the library. There they discovered there was a cave at the foot of the Acropolis with an opening that led up to the top. They found the opening and in the middle of the night climbed over some barbed wire, broke the lock, forced the door, then, using wood from an archaeological site, managed to climb up the shaft to the top of the Acropolis. They waited for the guards to move from their position, and then ran and cut the rope that held the swastika flag in place.

When Athens woke the next morning, they found that the flag symbolizing their oppression was gone. That day changed the course of Greek history, inspiring thousands of people to join the resistance. One of those inspired to join the fight was a 32-year-old shoemaker named Sokratis Skarlatos. He became a resistance fighter in the mountains, was captured and then escaped. He eventually moved to the US and settled there. His story and his life in turn inspired his grandson, Alek, who then went travelling around Europe with two of his friends, and when he got onto a train from Amsterdam to Paris, decided to run towards, rather than away from the man holding a gun with the intention of killing everyone on that train.

At that time when the Nazi regime seemed unstoppable, two teenagers went in the strength they had and an evil regime was eventually defeated. The Midianites seemed unstoppable, but this is their last mention as Israel's enemy in the Bible. This is their final defeat. There are many other forces in the world which seem unstoppable, but God calls ordinary, unremarkable people to go in the strength we have so that his extraordinary purposes might be fulfilled.

Chapter 8

LOVING

Ruth

Ruth 1 – 4

---

*But Ruth replied, 'Don't urge me to leave you or to turn back
from you. Where you go I will go, and where you stay I will stay.
Your people will be my people and your God my God. Where you
die I will die, and there I will be buried. May the LORD deal with
me, be it ever so severely, if even death separates you and me.'*

RUTH 1:16–17

You can't be sensible all the time.

LOVE ACTUALLY*

Thérèse of Lisieux joined a convent aged fifteen. She died nine
years later in 1897, aged just twenty-four. During her final illness
she overheard one of the other nuns saying, 'Sister Thérèse will
die soon; what will our Mother Prioress be able to write in her
obituary notice? She entered our convent, lived and died – there
really is no more to say.' However, through her autobiography, in
which she wrote about loving one another as Jesus loves us, she had
a significant impact on millions of people, becoming a saint in the
Catholic Church in 1925. Initially, having become a nun, Thérèse felt
overwhelmed by 'infinite desires', wanting to be a mother, a warrior,
a priest, an apostle, a doctor, a martyr, a papal guard and a prophet.
Then everything changed as she meditated on Paul's description of

---

* Richard Curtis, *Love Actually* (Universal Pictures, 2003).

love in 1 Corinthians 13. In her autobiography she described her realization:

> I understood that LOVE COMPROMISED ALL VOCATIONS, THAT LOVE WAS EVERYTHING, THAT IT EMBRACED ALL TIMES AND PLACES ... IN A WORD, THAT IT WAS ETERNAL!
>
> Then, in the excess of my delirious joy, I cried out: O Jesus, my Love ... my vocation, at last I have found it ... MY VOCATION IS LOVE!*

When I speak to people who are faced with a big decision about what to do with their lives, the conversation usually revolves around three elements: role, place and people. They tend to be trying to work out what they should be doing, where they should be doing it and with whom. In each case, one of these elements tends to become the main driving force for the decision about which path to take. For example, some people feel called to teach, and this is the main element of their calling, with questions of where they teach, and which school they work in, being secondary. Others feel called to a particular place. They know that they are meant to be in Zambia, for example, and then look for work and community in the place where God is calling them. In the Bible we see examples of each, for Abraham was primarily called to a particular place, whist Elijah was primarily called to a role.

However, in the book of Ruth we read the story of someone for whom the main driver is her calling to particular people, first to Naomi and then to Boaz, and where she goes and what she does flows from this. For Ruth the crucial question is 'whom am I supposed to love?'

As with many of these stories in the Bible, Ruth's calling emerges out of difficulty. The book of Ruth is placed immediately after the book of Judges and begins with the words, 'In the time of the Judges'. This is the period after Joshua has led the conquest of Canaan, but before their first king, Saul. It is a time characterized by chaos,

---

* Quoted in David F Ford, *The Shape of Living: Spiritual Directions for Everyday Life* (Baker Books, 2004), p100.

vulnerability and uncertainty, as the people of Israel are frequently attacked and enslaved by the nations around them. They are ruled by a series of leaders, many of them unreliable and flawed, and there is very little cohesion in society. Furthermore, here at the start of the book of Ruth we are told that they've recently gone through a time of economic hardship in the form of a famine (Ruth 1:1).

Ruth has been caught up in these national problems, having married one of the Israelite refugees who arrived in her homeland, Moab (1:4). In addition, she has had terrible personal problems. She has lost her husband (1:5). The life she had imagined for herself is gone. Not only is she grieving, but in a society where protection and provision depended on the men in your life, she is also now vulnerable, with the markers of identity and the structures of care removed from her life.

She was experiencing pain, disappointment and uncertainty about her future. And yet these things, instead of being obstacles to the fulfilment of God's purposes, become the fertile ground for God's grace and purposes. However, unlike some of the stories we've looked at, there is no audible voice, no visit from an angel, no sign from heaven to direct her path. There is simply a clear conviction of what she needs to do: to love the one in front of her.

When things are falling apart around you, when you're running out of options, when life feels tough and confusing, this is our calling: to love the ones in front of you. Ask yourself whom God has given you to love and then try to love them as well as you can.

LOVING THE ONE

Our purpose is to love God and love one another. And loving one another mostly means loving people one at a time. For love is not general, but specific. God loves the whole world, but he loves us individually. Jesus came into the world to demonstrate the love of God for the whole world, but so much of his ministry is focused on loving people one by one as he encounters them, healing a blind man, setting a demoniac free, raising a young girl back to life.

God is infinite and he loves all people infinitely. But our love is limited, by time and energy, and by the limitations of having bodies in one place at a time. Consequently, the greatest impact we can have in life is often through loving a few people well: husbands and wives, children and parents, friends and siblings, strangers in need or enemies who hate us.

In our first few years in Brighton there was a member of the congregation who was in recovery for addiction to alcohol. He had become involved in the life of the church, volunteering and making friends. But one day he wasn't at our Sunday morning service, and we were concerned, so we went round to his house where we were told that he had been collected by an ambulance. We went straight to the hospital where we found him with cuts on his face and heavily intoxicated. He had relapsed several days previously, and things had spiralled out of control for him.

We took him back to the worship pastor's house and made some calls. A group of us decided we would sit with him, praying for him non-stop until we could get him into rehab a few days later. People, some of whom barely knew him, dropped everything, giving up sleep, taking it in turns to sit and pray with him. These few days had a profound impact on him. He continued to struggle through the years and life was often tough, but he said he'd never experienced love quite like this.

During those days we were aware that there were so many people in Brighton in the same position as this young man and we couldn't do the same for everyone, but we operated on this principle: that we should do for the one what we wished we could do for everyone. We cannot always help everyone, but we can often help the person in front of us. When Jesus was asked what it meant to 'love your neighbour', he replied with the story of the Good Samaritan, which describes someone helping just one person in front of them whom they found in need.[*]

Sometimes loving the one in front of us is like the parable of

---

* Luke 10:30–35.

the Good Samaritan: loving someone for a short time to help them through a crisis. More often, as with marriage, parenting or looking after parents, it is a much longer commitment. Sometimes the one in front of us is a stranger; often it is someone we know well. Sometimes the one in front of us is someone people might expect us to love; at other times it is someone we could never imagine feeling called to help.

ENTERING THEIR WORLD

One way to love people is to invite them into our world. We might call this 'hospitality'. We open our homes to a stranger. We include a new person in our circle of friends. We draw people into our communities and activities. This is a good and beautiful way to love people. But what we see in Ruth is something even greater. For Ruth is willing to enter Naomi's world. Naomi's people are going to become Ruth's people, her country will become Ruth's country, her problems will become Ruth's problems (1:16–17). Ruth loves Naomi by identifying herself with her. What belongs to Naomi is going to belong to Ruth: her home, her priorities, her needs, her pain.

This is how God has loved us. He entered our world, identifying with our humanity, our lives, our problems. He will also draw us into his world, taking us to his house with many rooms,* but first he comes to us. He enters our world before we are brought into his.

Therefore, the essential skill for loving is the willingness to enter the other person's world, listening more than speaking, asking questions more than giving opinions. This is particularly true with children. I'm always keen to include my children in my interests, and will happily discuss with them sporting news, history, politics and current affairs. I find it much harder to enter their world and show interest in video games which make no sense to me, or make-believe worlds where you struggle to work out what is going on, but in which they are totally engrossed. But this is how we love people.

* John 14:2.

COMMITTING DESPITE REJECTION

We are called to love people with a commitment which endures even when we feel rejected by them. Ruth clings to Naomi (1:14). And she does this despite Naomi trying to persuade her to stay in Moab (1:15). Naomi appears to have the best intentions here. In many ways she is the model of how the older generations should relate to the younger generations: she tries to set Ruth free. Instead of insisting Ruth look after her, she tries to persuade Ruth to go back to her home country, to live her own life, to go her own path. But Ruth insists on staying with Naomi even when Naomi tells her to stay in her own country. Real commitment kicks in when we feel like the other is pushing us away.

Ruth has experienced so much heartbreak, losing her husband and everything that was tied up in that life that she had with him, that Naomi's attempt to send her away could easily have been taken as another rejection, communicating that she was not needed or wanted anymore. And yet Ruth refuses to let go of her. She clings to her. She commits to her, to death and even beyond death. She does this though her relationship lacks the usual bonds which bind people to each other permanently. Romance can create strong bonds, but they are not lovers. Blood can create strong bonds, but Naomi is not her parent, child or sister. And yet she commits herself completely to her mother-in-law.

It is powerful when someone commits to another person even when the other is pushing them away. We see this in the last hours of Elijah's life when the old prophet repeatedly tells his young assistant Elisha to stay where he is while he goes on alone. However, each time Elisha refuses to leave his side.* We see it when Joseph experienced the rejection he must have felt when he discovered that his fiancée Mary was pregnant, and he was not the father but is persuaded to commit to her nonetheless.** And we see it with Frodo and Sam in *The Lord of the Rings*. Frodo knows he must go to Mount Doom in Mordor, and believes he must go alone, but Sam has made a promise to go with him,

* 2 Kings 2:2, 4, 6.
** Matthew 1:24.

so he runs after Frodo, swimming to Frodo's boat and nearly drowning in the process. Frodo says to him, 'But I am going to Mordor.' And Sam replies, 'I know that well enough, Mr Frodo. Of course you are. And I'm coming with you.' Frodo replies, 'But I must go at once. It's the only way.' To which Sam responds, 'Of course it is … But not alone. I'm coming too, or neither of us isn't going. I'll knock holes in all the boats first.'*

For many years we felt this commitment to Archie and Sam Coates when we worked with them at St Peter's. This sense of commitment was so strong that at one point during our time in Brighton, Tara said to me, 'I know that there may come a time when you get a new vision, and feel like it's time to move on and sense that God is calling us elsewhere, and when that time comes, I want you to know that I'm staying here with Archie and Sam!'

Thankfully we made it to Brazil together. But in many ways, we ended up here in Rio because of a growing conviction that Tara was called to Brazil, and probably always has been, and my role is to come with her and refuse to leave her side here.

SACRIFICING EVERYTHING

In times of difficulty, we can often withdraw into ourselves, becoming self-absorbed, self-obsessed, trying to protect ourselves. Having recently lost her husband, Ruth could have focused on her own needs, asking, 'Who is going to look after me? How can I be cared for and protected?' However, instead she tries to work out how to look after her mother-in-law. In doing so Ruth is giving up so much. She is giving up the chance of marriage and having children. She is giving up her home and family. She's giving up the country she knows and loves. She's giving up the place where she knew the language and culture and how things worked. All for the sake of Naomi.

There is always an exchange in love. When you truly love someone

* JRR Tolkien, *The Lord of the Rings: The Fellowship of the Ring* (HarperCollins Publishers, 1995), p397.

there is always some kind of transfer. When your children are awake in the night, loving them means going without sleep to help them to sleep. If you have a friend who is finding life difficult, you meet up for coffee with them so that they can share their burdens, after which they tend to feel better, but you feel worse. When Tara and I got married my life was quite chaotic, and her life was very ordered. In getting married, Tara had to welcome into her life more chaos than she thought was possible, and I had to accept more order than I thought was necessary!

There is always an exchange. For Ruth to go with Naomi, Ruth has to be willing to become a foreigner. She gives up her own home so that the one she loved might find hers.

PRACTISING LOVE

We are called to love people practically. Loving Naomi will mean Ruth looking after her, going out into the fields to work and try to provide for her (2:2).

The psychiatrist, M. Scott Peck, in his bestseller, *The Road Less Travelled*, insists that 'Love is not a feeling',* commenting on our potential for self-deception because the feelings of love blind us to our lack of practical care for those people. You could have a father who feels like he loves his daughter, but does not provide for her, or remember her birthday, or know anything about her life, but thinks he loves her because he feels something for her. And you can have a mother who is struggling to bond with her baby boy, not feeling like she loves him, and yet feeding him, clothing him, protecting him, giving up her life for his benefit. Despite their feelings, the father does not really love his daughter whereas the mother really does love her son.

A few years ago I had a difficult conversation with a friend whose marriage was falling apart, and he wanted to see me to talk about what would happen to his wife if they got divorced. He told me

---

* M Scott Peck, *The Road Less Travelled* (Simon and Schuster, 2002), p116.

that he just didn't love her anymore. Maybe he'd never really loved her. But he wanted to talk to me because he was worried about her future. Who would look after her? What would happen with her job? What would be the impact of divorce on her life? And I looked at him, and said, 'You do love her. You've spent this whole time with me trying to work out how she is going to be OK. You love her more than you realize.'

I once came across a definition of love as 'the consistent feeling of joy in another's presence.' This might describe one element of love, which is delight in the other person. But this is not the love that the Bible describes, which is very often practical. When Jesus was asked to define what it meant to love your neighbour, he told the story of the Good Samaritan who loves a man he has never met before by stopping his journey, bandaging wounds, pouring oil and wine on them, lifting him onto his donkey, walking beside it while the man rode, taking care of him and paying his expenses.* Jesus loved the world by healing the sick, casting out demons and helping those in need. He demonstrated practical love. And the most loving person in history had the most practical of professions: he was a carpenter. So, I imagine him, even before he started his ministry, loving people by making them tables and chairs. The call to love is a call to love practically.

THE ADVENTURE OF LOVE

Ruth loves Naomi, and in doing so leaves her own country and sets out to a place she does not yet know. This is a demonstration of her love for her mother-in-law, but it points to something wider too: that all love means leaving your country in one sense or another. Whenever we truly love people, we are not just bringing people to where we are, no matter how beautiful a place that might be, nor simply going to where they are, good as that place might be. When

* Luke 10:33–35.

we love another person, each party 'must have the courage to go with them to a place that neither you nor they have ever been before."

This is true of marriage. It's true of having children. Children are not just absorbed into your life: you enter a new world which you've never experienced before. It's certainly true of becoming a pastor in a church in Rio de Janeiro. The pastor is not just absorbed into the community, nor the community absorbed into the pastor, but the pastor and the community go together to a new place which neither have known before.

LOVING BEYOND WHAT IS REASONABLE

Ruth demonstrates a love which goes beyond anything that could be expected of her. In this her sister-in-law, Orpah, provides a contrast. For Orpah operates totally reasonably. She is a good daughter-in-law, kind, responsible, respectful, devoted, but there is a limit. However, Ruth goes above and beyond what could be considered reasonable. It is an almost supernatural love, pointing to a greater love which would later come.

One of Ruth's descendants would be King David, from whose line would come the Messiah, Jesus, who left his home and came to another country, identifying with us completely, saying, in effect, to us, 'your world will be my world, your pain will be my pain, your guilt will be my guilt, your shame will be my shame, your death will be my death.' And then, through the letter of Paul to the Romans, reassures us so completely, that not even death would ever separate us (Romans 8:31–39). He commits to us completely, despite our rejection of him. He loves us practically, selflessly, sacrificially and endlessly.

This kind of love has a profound impact on those who are loved. Out of her pain Naomi says, 'Don't call me Naomi … Call me Mara' (1:20). Naomi's life has been so tough, it has affected her

* Vincent Donovan, *Christianity Rediscovered* (SCM Press, 2019), pvii.

whole identity. She chooses for herself a name that means 'bitter'. She defines herself based on what has happened to her and on what she feels. However, she doesn't get called 'Mara' throughout the rest of the book. Neither the narrator nor the other characters agree with her self-definition, for there was a love for Naomi which was stronger than her own attempts to define herself. We too have a love that is stronger than our own attempts to define ourselves. There is a love that secures our identity too.

And this is a love that gives hope for the future. The final words of the first chapter in Ruth mention that 'the barley harvest was beginning' (1:22). Out of the ashes of grief and disappointment, the harvest was coming. There is a love that brings new life out of the ashes.

This love for the one in front of us has a significance beyond what we can expect. Ruth is a foreigner, operating in an obscure part of Israel, not connected to the great events of the age. She is quiet, on the edge, and her story is undramatic in many ways, consisting of the things of normal life: collecting food, getting married, births and deaths. Yet her devotion to Naomi, and then to Boaz, pulls her into the story of King David, her great-grandson, who will be the greatest king of Israel. And through David, Ruth is linked in the long chain of descendants to Jesus himself. Because of her simple acts of kindness and devotion to one or two people, in obscure parts of the world, she gets to appear in the genealogies of the Messiah.*

This is the great calling on our lives: to love, as best we can, practically and sacrificially, the ones God puts in front of us.

* Matthew 1:5.

Chapter 9

LISTENING

Samuel

1 Samuel 3

---

*The LORD came and stood there, calling as at the other times,
'Samuel! Samuel!'*
Then Samuel said, 'Speak, for your servant is listening.'

1 SAMUEL 3:10

I was sure it was God's voice. I was certain that He was calling
me. The message was clear: I must leave the convent to help the
poor by living among them. This was a command, something to
be done, something definite. I knew where I had to be. But I did
not know how to get there.

MOTHER TERESA*

A life of purpose needs inspiration. These biblical characters who
are called by God receive their calling by hearing God's voice,
whether it is through an audible voice (as with Moses) or an inner
conviction (as with Ruth), whether it is through signs (Gideon),
dreams (Joseph) or something more subtle and intangible. Calling
emerges from hearing. God calls us by speaking to us. The story
of Samuel is one in which a boy begins to hear God's voice, and
through hearing God's voice begins to discover God's purpose for
his life. But how do we hear God's voice? And how do we know that
we've got it right when we do?

* Quoted in Ruth Tucker, *Extraordinary Women of Christian History: What We Can
Learn from Their Struggles and Triumphs* (Baker Publishing Group, 2016), p462.

START WITH PROXIMITY

The first step in hearing God's voice is to draw close to God. Of course, God can speak to us at any time and in any place, interrupting us when we are trying to ignore him or run from him. But God often speaks as we draw close to him. God spoke to Moses when he approached his presence in the burning bush, to Elijah when he went up Mount Horeb and to Isaiah when he was in the temple. We cannot make God speak to us, but we can seek proximity to God.

Samuel 'was lying down in the house of the LORD' (3:2) when God spoke to him. He was in the place of the presence of God, in the place where God spoke to people. We cannot control God, insisting that he give us the answers that we want about the direction of our lives. We cannot force God to speak, but we can put ourselves in the place where God speaks.

It says that 'in those days the word of the LORD was rare' (3:1). Maybe you feel the same. It might feel like God's voice is rare, or even like you are not sure if you've ever heard God's voice. In those times, the best thing we can do is keep going back to the places where God speaks, staying in the presence of God no matter what.

So firstly, and most importantly, we find ways to read the Bible, spending time each day in God's presence so that he can speak to us. There might be times when each morning reading the Bible is filled with delight as we sense God guiding us and challenging us and comforting us with his Word. At other times it may feel like hard work, and it's difficult to know what God might be saying. But as we read the Bible each day it keeps us in the presence of the one who is always speaking to us through his Word.

When trying to discern God's voice for our lives, it is beneficial to spend a sustained time in his presence. Samuel was sleeping in the house of God when God spoke to him. He was spending hours in God's presence. After prolonged periods spent with God, he hears a voice calling him clearly.

Whenever I have had to make particularly important decisions, like whether to propose to Tara or whether to move to Brazil, I have taken a few days to pray and fast, to spend time with God and listen to his voice. Those times have not usually included dramatic moments of hearing God's voice or knowing what to do next. Mostly, I spent those days feeling hungry and looking forward to my next meal! However, looking back, I can see that the big changes in my life, times when I have sensed greater clarity for the direction of my life, have followed those times.

William Wilberforce was a British Member of Parliament who had a radical conversion to Christianity at the end of the eighteenth century. Soon after he became an MP the direction of his life changed dramatically. He was a transformed man, emerging with a deep, unshakeable conviction about the immorality of slavery and the moral character of his nation. However, this conversion did not take place in one dramatic moment. His conversion was radical but gradual. His sense of calling was totally clear, but unlike some others like him, there is no record of a vision, a blinding light or a defining moment. However, Wilberforce meditated on the Bible every day. He placed God's Word at the centre of his life, so that he lived under the continual inspiration of God's voice. This is what shaped his purpose in a clear and powerful way.*

RECEIVE IT PERSONALLY

God has a unique purpose for your life. When God calls Samuel, it is not general, but specific. God calls him by name (3:6, 8, 10). He calls, 'Samuel, Samuel' not 'Anyone, anyone'. He is not asking a crowd for any volunteers but calling a specific person for a specific role. God calls you by name. God has a unique purpose for your life, based on his knowledge of who you are.

When I was growing up, I used to hear stories of Brother Andrew,

* Eric Metaxas, *Amazing Grace* (HarperCollins, 2007), p221.

about how he smuggled Bibles to persecuted and isolated Christians in communist countries during the Cold War. But it was only much later when I read his book, *God's Smuggler*, that I discovered what kind of person he was. I particularly enjoyed the stories from his childhood. He used to play practical jokes on his neighbours, putting panes of glass on their chimneys so that their houses filled with smoke. He would skip church to go ice-skating, sneaking back just before the end of the service to try to pick up what people said about the sermon, so that he could talk about it with confidence with his family over lunch. Then, when the Nazis invaded in the 1940s he would sneak out, aged only ten years old, and put sugar in the engine of the army lieutenant, or launch fireworks at them, then run across the fields and hide. Brother Andrew was a rebel, a natural lawbreaker and risk-taker. That is how God had made him, and when later he called him, it was because he knew him personally, and God intended to channel his character towards a great purpose.

God called Samuel because he knew Samuel. Samuel's name is significant. It means 'heard by God.' It refers to his family history, which was complicated. His father, Elkanah, had two wives, resulting in jealousy and competition between these two women. Samuel's mother, Hannah, had endured years of not being able to conceive, until God eventually answered her prayer. Almost all families are complicated in some way, and they are an important part of who we are. God knows your history and has a purpose to work through it. Your parents' strengths and weaknesses, their successes and failures, are not obstacles to the purposes that God has for you. For he calls you by name, knowing your family history, your gifts, your character and your brokenness. Your brokenness is part of the uniqueness of who you are, and part of God's purpose for your life.

DRAW ON THE COMMUNITY

God is always speaking, more than we realize. God speaks to Samuel before he knows that it is God. But he needs help from those around him to hear and recognize that it is God's voice. Samuel's call is personal, but it is worked out in community.

It starts with his mother Hannah who took her prayer for a child to the place where God would hear her, the tabernacle. She recognized that family life, marriage and having children are not just about our self-fulfilment and forming the lifestyle we want but are all part of the purposes of God. For Hannah, it was more important that her prayer had been heard by God, and that she then kept the vow she had made, than that she kept the child she had longed for with her. For Hannah, it was equally important that Samuel was in the place where he could hear God's voice for himself.

As a parent, I know that I cannot force my children to have faith in Jesus. I cannot make them have a relationship with God, but I can keep bringing them into the presence of God, to the places where God speaks, reading the Bible with them, praying with them, drawing them into the life of the church, and asking that God would begin to speak to them. Some the most wonderful times we have had as a family have been when we have tried to listen to God's voice together. On a few occasions the things which God has said to our children have changed the course of our lives.

Samuel hears God's voice, first because he has been brought to the temple by his mother, but then because Eli helps him to discern the voice of God for himself. I imagine this was a bit of a pain for Eli, being woken up repeatedly in the middle of the night, and we can sense the annoyance the first couple of times that Samuel comes to him. But, eventually, Eli is willing to go without some sleep to help young Samuel learn to hear the voice of God. He doesn't put himself in between Samuel and God, offering to hear God's voice on Samuel's behalf. He teaches Samuel how to hear God's voice for himself. Eli helps Samuel to recognize God's voice, and then he draws the word of God out of him.

Eli does this with a mixture of reassurance and insistence. He says 'Samuel, my son' (3:16), calling him by name, reminding him that he is like a son to him. He shows him that he is safe and loved. But he also senses that Samuel might hold himself back without some prompting, so he is also forceful in his tone with him, insisting, 'What was it he said to you?' and then demanding, 'Do not hide it from me. May God deal with you, be it ever so severely, if you hide from me anything he told you' (3:17). It is this combination of reassuring him and making him feel safe, and challenging him to do what he might not naturally do, which enables Samuel to learn to hear the voice of God.

Interestingly, it appears that Eli was not in the habit of hearing God's voice for himself, for 'in those days the word of the LORD was rare; there were not many visions' (3:1) and yet he was able to help Samuel even with something outside of his own experience. Eli was much older than Samuel, was almost blind, and didn't have personal experience of hearing God's voice, and yet he was still able to help him. And it will come at a cost to Eli, for helping Samuel to hear God's voice for himself will be part of God's plans in which Samuel will eventually take the place of Eli's family. Eli will be succeeded by Samuel, not by his sons. But even so, he is willing to help Samuel to take hold of God's purpose for him and to take his own place as Israel's leader.

The church is a community of people who help one another to hear God's voice, and help one another to align ourselves with God's purpose for us. We can help one another even when we are at different stages of life, when our spiritual life is different to those we are helping, and when it comes at a cost to us personally. And then those who have been helped by older generations can help the next generation too. Eli helped Samuel, and when Samuel was older, he would discover another young boy called David, and just as Eli had helped him, Samuel would help David to discover his calling as the next king of Israel (1 Samuel 16).

We look to the generation above not to give us the answers, but to help us hear God's voice and work out our purpose, and we look to the generation below to help them in their purpose. We honour our parents, and we teach our children. We learn from the generation above and release the generation below.

Moses helped Joshua discover his purpose. Elizabeth would help Mary. Even Jesus would go to the temple and listen to and ask questions of the generation above, and then train and send out his disciples. William Wilberforce did not work out his purpose on his own. It was only together with his great friend Pitt the Younger, the much older and wiser John Newton, who had written the hymn *Amazing Grace*, Thomas Clarkson, Zachary Macaulay, Hannah More and the other members of the Clapham Sect. It was the people around him who encouraged him, challenged him, and helped him to work out his purpose. Our purpose is shaped by community and fulfilled through community.

LEAN INTO UNCERTAINTY

It is easy to miss, but there is, perhaps, something significant in the way in which Samuel tries to follow Eli's advice. Eli tells Samuel to say, 'Speak, LORD, for your servant is listening' (3:9). But Samuel says, 'Speak, for your servant is listening' (3:10). He doesn't address God as 'LORD,' possibly because he is still not sure who is speaking to him.

However, even without being sure, he opens himself up to the voice he is beginning to recognize. He leans into the uncertainty. It is not always easy to know whether it is God speaking to us, and what God might want from us. Of course, there are some things we can be certain of: that God loves us, and that he is faithful, that Jesus will return one day. But whether to marry a particular person, or to take a particular job, or to move to Brazil – these things are harder to know for certain.

It is always difficult to have certainty when we are dealing with the voice of God guiding our steps. Admittedly, there are stories, both in the Bible and in Church history, of angels, audible voices, divine visitations and clear signs, as God directs our steps according to his purpose. But for most of us, most of the time, we are simply trying to do our best with the information that we have, and it can all feel quite unclear. We should always be aware that we might be misled by our own wishful thinking, or our imagination, or the internalized voice of our parents or culture. Listening to God always involves a degree of uncertainty. And we can feel paralysed by the uncertainty, terrified of getting it wrong. But if we waited until we were certain, we would never do anything.

On 3 January 2009, Tara and I went down from London to Brighton for a day trip. We had been dating for a year, and I was planning on proposing that day. I had asked her parents for permission a few weeks before and they had gladly given it. Everything was planned for the day. We would go and see St Peter's, the church we thought God might be leading us to join, we would walk along the beach, and then I would propose using a sapphire that I had bought and could be put in an engagement ring.

However, two days before our trip to Brighton, Tara and I were having dinner and Tara told me that she'd been having nightmares. 'About what?' I asked her. 'About you proposing,' she replied. 'I suppose I'm worried that you're going to be ready before I am.'

Bearing in mind all my planning, that was a bit discouraging. I started asking myself, 'Have I got this all wrong?' Then, on 3 January, I woke up feeling ill, and so I decided to cancel our day trip. There was no harm in delaying the proposal. I would give Tara some more time to be ready.

However, before I sent her a message to cancel our trip, I spent some time reading the Bible and listening to God's voice. That morning the reading for the day was about the baptism of Jesus in the Jordan, where I read that 'John tried to deter him ... but Jesus replied, "Let it be so now; it is proper for us to do this to fulfil all righteousness." Then John consented." It felt like something hit me as I read these verses, and I sensed God say that I should propose that day. I was aware that this could be wishful thinking. But I thought I would at least go through with the day and see how things went.

So, we travelled down to Brighton on the train. We visited St Peter's and our hearts leapt as we saw it. We felt this was somewhere God might be calling us both together. We walked along the seafront, talking happily about the future. I showed her the house I used to come to each summer with my family for our summer holidays. We sat down on the beach and had a picnic. The sun was shining; it was unseasonably warm. The setting was perfect. So, I asked Tara to marry me.

She didn't say 'yes'. In fact, she burst into tears. And then we began to talk about how we could know whether this was the right thing to do. She asked me, 'How do you know for certain that this is right?' And I replied, 'I don't know for certain. But Martin Luther said that the quest for certainty is unbelief.'** I'm not sure whether quoting Reformation theologians is the most romantic way to persuade someone to marry you, but it worked. And four and half hours after my first proposal I asked Tara again, and this time she said, 'Yes.' And then I burst into tears.

Faith means we are never quite certain, but we lean into the uncertainty. In the story of the Great Commission at the end of Matthew's Gospel, it says that the disciples 'went where Jesus had told them to go. When they saw him, they worshipped him; but some doubted.'*** Even after seeing the resurrected Jesus there is still some doubt. And it is in the context of this uncertainty that

* Matthew 3:14–15.
** Though convinced at the time that I was correctly quoting Martin Luther, I have since discovered that Luther didn't say this, nor have I been able to find out who did. I am grateful that God worked through this conversation despite my poor referencing.
*** Matthew 28:16–17.

Jesus sends them out to make disciples of all nations. The greatest moment of calling in the history of the world was done in the context of doubt. They had their doubts, but crucially they were still there. And their purpose emerged in the uncertainty. If you wait for certainty, you might find yourself waiting forever. But if you lean into the uncertainty you will begin to be filled with the inspiration that will fuel your purpose.

Here Samuel starts responding to God with a degree of uncertainty, but he would later learn to hear God so clearly that when he was older God would bring him before a man called Jesse, who had eight sons, and tell him to anoint one of them as the next king. And as each came before him, he knew with absolute certainty, 'not that one, not that one, not that one …' until finally David came forward and he knew for sure (16:1–13). He started when he was uncertain and then spent years learning to listen with more and more confidence to the voice of God.

This is the beginning of Samuel discovering his purpose. But though God speaks to him, he doesn't call him to a specific role or to fulfil a specific task. He doesn't say to him, 'You are going to be a prophet, or a judge, or king' or 'you need to defeat the Philistines and restore peace to Israel.' He simply starts speaking to him. So often we are searching for a position or a goal to aim for, but purpose is not found in a title or a role, but in God's voice and God's presence. If you live in God's presence and listen to God's voice, then you will live a life of purpose. For calling is not a one-off event, but a continuous journey of listening to the voice of God.

Of all the prophetic words given to me, one of the most helpful was from an older Christian who prayed for me when I was twenty-two years old and trying to work out what to do with my life. He told me that God would guide me with a compass and not a map. I wouldn't need to see the whole route ahead of me, but he would show me the right direction as I walked with him.

This story of calling ends with the words, 'The LORD was with

Samuel as he grew up, and he let none of Samuel's words fall to the ground' (3:19). It literally says, 'and he did not let any of his words fall to the ground.' The Hebrew is unclear as to whether it is referring to Samuel not letting God's words fall to the ground, God not letting Samuel's words fall to the ground, or God not letting God's words fall to the ground. Each of these options are encouraging and challenging in their own way, but I particularly love the third. The image is like that of a parent throwing a ball to a young child and then helping them to catch it. Naturally we miss God's voice, ignore God's voice, forget his voice or misinterpret his voice. But here is the hope that God will not only speak to us but also help us to catch what he says, so that we can live our lives inspired by him and called by him.

For Samuel the inspiration of his life was God's voice which he was learning to listen to, but for us today we have something greater and clearer. We have the cross of Jesus Christ. This is the reminder of the death and resurrection of Jesus Christ, the clear evidence that we are eternally and unconditionally loved by God, the reassurance that our sins are forgiven, that death is defeated, that Jesus Christ is our Saviour and that he is alive today. Of all the inspirations that could drive our purpose, I can think of nothing greater than the cross of Jesus Christ, which has been the inspiration for so many people for so many centuries, those who have given their lives in the service of the one who died for us.

Chapter 10

FACING PROBLEMS AND TAKING OPPORTUNITIES

David

1 Samuel 17

As he was talking with them, Goliath, the Philistine champion from Gath, stepped out from his lines and shouted his usual defiance, and David heard it.

1 SAMUEL 17:23

Be very careful, then, how you live – not as unwise but as wise, making the most of every opportunity, because the days are evil.

EPHESIANS 5:15–16

Westley: A few more steps and we'll be safe in the fire swamp.
Buttercup: We'll never survive!
Westley: Nonsense. You're only saying that because no one
ever has.

THE PRINCESS BRIDE*

At school I played a little bit of rugby. I wasn't very fast, or strong. And I didn't really like being tackled. Or tackling. Or kicking. But I loved rugby, and my favourite position was 'fly half', because from

---

* Rob Reiner, *The Princess Bride* (Twentieth Century Fox, 1987).

there I got to dictate the game. I got to decide what we would do and which side we went to. Before the ball came to me, I would call a 'move', which was a particular plan of attack. But as I received the ball, sometimes a gap would open up in front of me just as I was about to pass, and then I would abandon the move, and try to take the opportunity that had emerged.

Life is a combination of plans and opportunities. We make plans and we take opportunities. Goliath was not part of David's own plan for his life. He was a shepherd and messenger, and he had also been anointed as future king. Killing giants was not part of the plan. But here an opportunity emerges and David takes it.

A life of purpose combines both plans and opportunities. It is good to make plans, to think where you want to be in five years' time, to have goals and targets. It is good to make plans; but it is essential to take opportunities.

These opportunities often come in the form of problems. Life will always be filled with various kinds of problems, and these can sometimes feel like they are preventing us from doing the things we should be doing. They might appear to interfere with our calling. However, very often the problems we face are themselves the work which God has given us to do. They are opportunities to fulfil our purpose.

Here David is faced with a very large, well-armed, self-confident, violent and aggressive problem called Goliath. This was a large problem, for it carried the risk of defeat and destruction of the new nation. It was an insoluble problem, for neither the current king, Saul, nor any of the Israelites had a solution. It was a long-term problem, for it had lasted forty days with no sign of a breakthrough. And it was a stressful problem, filling the Israelites with 'great fear' (1 Samuel 17:24) and 'dismay' (17:11). They felt disheartened, losing hope and wanting to give up. But what everyone else saw as a problem David sees as an opportunity. We can either go through life seeing problems as problems, or we can see problems as opportunities.

One possible reason that David sees the problem differently from everyone else was that he is an outsider. The Israelite army had been facing this problem for a while and could see no way through it, but David comes to it from the outside, as someone who might appear like he doesn't belong. His outsider perspective enables him to see the problem as an opportunity. This might be why God often calls people to new places. He calls Abraham to move to Canaan (rather than choosing a Canaanite), he calls Moses to go back to Egypt only after he fled in disgrace (rather than calling him while he was still in Pharoah's court) and he calls David here (rather than one of the soldiers who has been facing the giant every day for the last month). Outsiders can sometimes see opportunities where the rest of us have simply accepted them as problems that are a part of life and will never change.

So, David will see this problem as an opportunity. In contrast, King Saul will take this same opportunity – as David comes out of the battle as a brilliant warrior and leader who is totally loyal to Saul – and turn it into a problem. David is the greatest opportunity to emerge during Saul's reign, but Saul's insecurity and jealousy will mean that he only sees David as a problem. Whereas David saw a problem as an opportunity; Saul will see an opportunity as a problem. We can either go through life seeing problems as opportunities, or we can see opportunities as problems.

A life of purpose is one where we turn problems into opportunities. The problems or issues you are facing right now might not be an obstacle to you fulfilling your purpose, but the very means of you fulfilling your purpose. For our purpose is to confront and challenge and overcome the problems that come our way. Life is a series of opportunities coming in the form of battles, opposition and difficulty. We are called to turn whatever we are facing – personally, nationally, culturally – into an opportunity. A purpose-filled life is one in which every stage of life, every experience of life, in work or out of work, studying or retired, healthy or sick, whether we are single or married, with young children or teenage children or no children, from being a problem to being an opportunity.

RUNNING TOWARDS THE PROBLEM

First, we must run towards the problem. The Israelites run away from Goliath (17:24) but David runs towards him (17:48). We can try to avoid problems, ignore them or deny them. But our purpose is found when we move towards rather than away from them. This is true of global problems, like inequality, racism, injustice, modern slavery, hunger, loneliness, climate change; it is also true of the problems we face personally and internally.

It's easy to conclude that the problems around us must be someone else's job. It would have been perfectly reasonable for David to think that this was Saul's problem to sort out. After all, Saul was their biggest warrior, a head taller than any of the others, so surely he should be the one fighting the tallest Philistine. He was also the king. David could legitimately feel like Saul should show some leadership and confront Goliath himself. He could have spent his time trying to persuade the king that this was his problem, maybe even starting a campaign or a petition to try to get him to take more responsibility. But David decided that he would face this problem himself.

As we step forward ourselves, and as we move towards the problem, we do so not in strength but in vulnerability. David takes off the armour to fight Goliath (17:39). He runs towards him unprotected, defenceless and vulnerable. He is physically vulnerable, but he is also emotionally vulnerable. David appears self-confident here, but when we read about the rest of his life and the psalms he wrote, the striking feature of his character is not his bravery but his brokenness.

We also move towards the problems we face when we fight them differently from the way the world deals with problems. When David refuses Saul's armour, he is refusing to fight as Saul would fight (17:39). But more significantly it means that he refuses to fight as Goliath fights. Goliath wore armour; David would not.

The battles we face tend to drag us into the same methods of warfare as those who fight against us. If people lie about us, we are tempted to respond with lies about them. If people gossip about us, we can find ourselves complaining to other people about the gossipers (failing to recognize that this too is gossip). If we notice people trying to cling on to power, we can find ourselves trying to work out how to maintain power for ourselves.

But we are called to fight differently from the way the world fights. Later in the Old Testament, when the Jewish exile Daniel becomes the highest-ranking official in the Persian Empire, he discovers that his colleagues have come up with a scheme to trap him, have him stripped of his power and thrown to the lions. Given his position and abilities he could easily have responded with a counter-scheme, to trap them, rob them of their power and have them thrown to the lions. Instead, he goes home, gets on his knees and prays, letting himself be caught and thrown to the lions. He fights his battle on his knees, and lets God fight his political battles.*

Paul would later write, 'For though we live in the world, we do not wage war as the world does.'** We fight these battles with more confidence and with more vulnerability, running towards the problems instead of away from them.

CONFOUNDING THE CRITICS

As soon as we move towards the problem, we will experience criticism. The bigger the problem and the more courageously we run towards it, the more likely we are to face opposition. There will almost always be critics.

In this story David is frequently criticized and attacked. His brother Eliab attacks his character, telling him that he's 'conceited' and 'wicked' (17:28). And David's reply of, 'Now what have I done?'

* Daniel 6.
** 1 Corinthians 10:3.

suggests that he is criticized frequently at home. After all, he is the youngest sibling. Saul then attacks his ability, telling him he's too young, that he doesn't have the skill or experience to defeat Goliath (17:33). Saul also criticizes his method, dressing him in his armour and trying to get him to do it how he would do it (17:38). It's a subtle form of that frequent criticism, 'It's not *what* you're trying to do, it's the *way* you're doing it that's wrong.' Finally, Goliath attacks his spirit, calling down curses on him (17:43).

David receives criticism from his family, from his superiors and from his enemies. It comes from people who are trying to help and people who are trying to defeat him. Some is aggressive; some is subtle. We will always get criticism whenever we are trying to do anything significant. But David confounds his critics. He refuses to be crushed by criticism. He's not going to be defined by the opinions of others or let the views of others distract him from his purpose.

A few years ago, Tara received some harsh criticism. There were a couple of voices telling her that she couldn't do something, and she rose up and defeated them, crushing them completely. The voices happened to be from two of our children, who told her that they thought they would beat her easily at football. They re-emerged from the garden 10 minutes later looking broken and dejected to say that 'Mummy beat us 7-0'. Tara feels it's important for our children not to be shielded from the harsh realities of life!

When we are criticized, we have to decide who we are going to listen to. David 'turns away' from Eliab, he counters Saul's objection to him fighting, he refuses Saul's armour and he ignores Goliath's curses. We cannot stop the critics, but we can decide who we listen to.

And with criticism comes another opportunity. When David is told by Saul that he won't be able to do it, it reminds him of what has happened in the past, of how God has been with him before, and this stirs his faith that he can do it again (17:34–37). As he tries on Saul's armour, his discomfort in it clarifies for him the correct way that he should fight Goliath and he emerges with confidence about his strategy (17:39–40). When Goliath calls down curses on him, it draws out of him a greater faith and vision for what is going to take place (17:45–47). Criticism of his ability brings out his faith, criticism of his method brings about clarity of his strategy and the curses directed at him only increase his confidence in God.

As someone who is quite sensitive, I tend to get discouraged easily by criticism, getting overwhelmed when attacked. I much prefer it when everyone says lots of encouraging things to me and everyone else and we all get on. But, looking back, the criticisms we've received in Rio have helped shape our vision and strategy here. When people insisted the church should only be for the British, it became clearer that we are meant to have a vision for all the nations. When we were criticized for our focus on the poor, we became more convinced that we needed to follow the example of the one who preached good news to the poor. Through the criticism, the vision and the strategy became clearer and stronger.

REASSESSING THE PAST

Turning problems into opportunities requires us to reassess our own pasts. David can confront the problem that he is facing because of the way that he understands his own past. He is confident he can overcome Goliath because in his mind this has happened before. He says,

> Your servant has been keeping his father's sheep. When a lion or a bear came and carried off a sheep from the flock, I went after it, struck it and rescued the sheep from its mouth. When it turned on me, I seized it by its hair, struck it and rescued the sheep from its mouth. Your servant has killed both the lion and the bear; this uncircumcised Philistine will be like one of them, because he has defied the armies of the living God. The LORD who rescued me from the paw of the lion and the paw of the bear will rescue me from the hand of this Philistine.

1 SAMUEL 17:34–37

As David looks back through his life, he sees repeated examples of God's deliverance. He sees the present battle in the context of past battles.

It is striking that David connects facing the Philistine Goliath with the challenges he has faced in the past, for there isn't necessarily a link between fighting heavily armed giants and protecting sheep from wild animals. I'm not an expert in single combat (nor in fighting wild animals), but I would imagine that bears and lions present a different set of challenges to giants. Bears and lions don't tend to be armed, for example. David might easily have said to himself, 'This is unlike anything I've had to fight before. I've fought wild animals, but I could never fight a giant with a huge spear.'

However, he sees his life as one in which God has delivered him time and again. This is not the only way that he could have interpreted his life. He was the youngest of eight sons, often forgotten, and not invited when his father held parties for distinguished guests. He had to work as a shepherd, spending long days on his own. There were several occasions when he had been attacked by wild animals and almost died. And his brothers frequently criticized him. He could have seen his life as one in which he was always mistreated and everything seemed to go wrong. Instead, he saw it as one in which God had intervened again and again to save him.

I'll never forget when I heard a friend say in a talk she gave at St Peter's, 'Of course I'm lucky, because I'm adopted, and so I've always known that I was loved and wanted.' That is not the only way for her to have interpreted her story, but that is how she has seen her past.

I know that I can look back on having chronic fatigue in my twenties and see it as a time of loss. When most people my age were most full of life and energy and at their most social, I was particularly tired and inactive and at times isolated. I could look back on everything I missed out on. Or I can look back on that time as when God taught me the beauty of limitations, where I learnt that I was loved without having to do anything, where I discovered new friends, new depths, read lots of books and watched a lot of high-quality TV series.

When we become Christians, God not only enters our present and helps us to reimagine our future, but he also invades our pasts, enabling us to see what has happened in a different light. And this is what gives us the confidence to face the battles in front of us.

GOING DOWN INTO THE VALLEY

The Israelites are on one hill, with the Philistines on the other, and so for David to defeat Goliath he must go down into the valley. I wonder whether David was thinking of this when he composed Psalm 23 and described going down into the valley of the shadow of death. When God calls us, it is inevitable that we will have to go down into a valley. Moses had to go back to the place of his failure to a people who didn't want him to lead them. Jonah would have to go to the depths of the sea. Daniel would have to go into the lion's den. Esther would have to risk her life by going unsummoned to the king. There is no way to avoid the valley.

JRR Tolkien saw this clearly. In *The Lord of the Rings*, each of the Christ-like characters has to face some kind of death: Gandalf has to face the Balrog, Aragorn has to go through the paths of the dead, Frodo has to go to Mount Doom. We cannot avoid the valley.

Jesus himself would need to go to the cross. Again and again he told his disciples that, for him to fulfil his purpose, he would need to be arrested, tortured and killed. He told them that they would have to follow a similar path if they wanted to be his disciples. It was one of the hardest things for the disciples to grasp. This is one of the hardest things for us to accept. Everything in us tells us to avoid the valley, to run from the valley. But God calls us to fulfil our calling by going through the valley.

Before he fought Goliath, David was anointed by Samuel and the power of the Holy Spirit came upon him (16:13). The Spirit of God was the driving force which propelled him towards the problem instead of away from it. The Spirit of God steadied him and secured him despite so much criticism. The Spirit of God was the inspiration which enabled him to see the link between past battles and the present challenge. And the Spirit of God led him into the valley and through the other side.

And, of course, David points ahead to one far greater who would take on the problems which we could never solve for ourselves. Jesus is the one who ran towards the great enemy: of sin, suffering and death, who endured mockery and ridicule to do so, and who transformed all our pasts, all our presents, all our futures in the process. He is the one who has faced all battles for us, and who makes it possible for us to face the problems in front of us.

Chapter 11

ACCEPTING CHANGE AND GETTING CLARITY

Nehemiah

Nehemiah 1 – 2

When I heard these things, I sat down and wept. For some days I mourned and fasted and prayed before the God of heaven.

NEHEMIAH 1:4

I love it when a plan comes together.

THE A-TEAM*

Calling requires change; sometimes in small and hidden ways, sometimes in huge and obvious ways, transforming every part of our lives: where we live, what we do and how we operate. This change comes even when we're not looking for it.

Nehemiah was not apparently looking for change. He was doing well in his profession. He had a senior role in the king's court in Persia with a high level of responsibility. He was trusted, serving the king of the most powerful empire in the world. But suddenly everything changed. He moved from Susa to Jerusalem, leaving behind his role as cupbearer at the capital to become a provincial governor, working alongside an entirely new group of people. It was a total change.

---

* Frank Lupo, Stephen J Cannell, *The A Team* (Universal Television, 1983–1987).

However, unlike the dramatic changes which took place when God called Abraham, Moses or Gideon, there is no account of God speaking directly or clearly to Nehemiah. There is no record of a dream, no angelic visitation nor a voice from heaven. The dramatic transformation of his life comes without a dramatic encounter with God. Yet Nehemiah is willing to embrace this change.

And he is willing to accept huge change because a new purpose for his life comes to light. His sense of calling, though not coming out of a direct encounter with God, nevertheless takes shape. He begins to get clarity. He grows in confidence about what God is asking him to do. He comes up with a plan.

This new direction and clear sense of what to do next develops from five crucial elements which come together to shape calling and take lives in whole new directions.

PASSION

It all starts with tears. Nehemiah writes, 'When I heard these things, I sat down and wept' (Nehemiah 1:4). God breaks his heart so that he can redirect his purpose. From these tears, he becomes sure that God has called him and is leading him in a new direction: he is now confident about what 'God had put in my heart to do for Jerusalem' (2:12).

One of the features of our transition from Brighton to Brazil was lots of tears. As a teenager, whenever Tara heard about Brazil she would begin to cry. And when we started to consider Brazil again, talking about it with friends and family, we often found ourselves inexplicably in tears, sometimes uncontrollably and in ways which I imagine were both confusing and embarrassing for those we were talking to!

One of the indicators that God might be speaking to you is the presence of tears. For our purpose emerges from our passion. This is not quite the same as the common advice to 'follow your heart' or 'find something you're passionate about', because our natural passions are complicated. Our passions, like our bodies, our minds, our desires and our emotions, are all fallen, a mixture of good and evil. Sometimes our passions are to be famous, comfortable or significant. So simply following our passions is not enough. Instead, we need to allow God to give us his heart, letting the passions of God become our passions.

One night in the 1950s, the country pastor David Wilkerson was reading *Life* magazine, when he came across the story of a trial of seven teenagers for the murder of a boy with polio. He describes what happened in *The Cross and the Switchblade*:

> My attention was caught by the eyes of one of the figures in the drawing. A boy. One of seven boys on trial. For murder. The artist had caught such a look of bewilderment and hatred and despair in his features that I opened the magazine wide again to get a closer look. And as I did, I began to cry.

Out of those tears God spoke to David Wilkerson, 'Go to New York City and help those boys.' It was the beginning of a whole new direction for his life. Though he was a rural preacher with no experience or knowledge of those children, nor the gang culture in New York, he managed to raise some money from his sceptical congregation to go to New York to see if he could meet these teenagers.

Getting into his car with his youth pastor, Miles, with everyone thinking he was crazy, consumed with doubts and fears, he asked Miles to open the Bible at random and put his finger on a verse and read it to him (knowing that this is not how you're supposed to read the Bible). Miles did this and then read out the verse he had his finger on, from Psalm 126, 'They that sow in tears shall reap in joy. He that goeth forth and weepeth, bearing precious seed, shall doubtless come again with rejoicing, bringing his sheaves with him.'* Then he writes, 'We were greatly encouraged as we drove on

---

* Psalm 126:5–6, KJV.

toward New York. And it was a good thing, because it was the last encouragement we were to receive for a long, long time."

Through tears God ensures that our calling goes beneath the surface. He breaks our hearts to place a passion deep within them. God's purpose for our lives will always be tested and challenged. There will be distractions, discouragements and disappointments. And so God plants his concerns deep within our hearts so that we will be able to weather these storms. It is through tears and broken hearts that God's purpose is planted deep within us. So let God break your heart and give his passion to you.

KNOWLEDGE

Passion alone is insufficient. Nehemiah's calling is nurtured, not only by a new passion, but also by new information. He writes,

> *Hanani, one of my brothers, came from Judah with some other men, and I questioned them about the Jewish remnant that had survived the exile, and also about Jerusalem.*

NEHEMIAH 1:2

Through this conversation he investigates the situation back at home, and then later, once he gets to Jerusalem, he examines the state of the city, particularly its walls and gates. New information breaks his heart, and then his passion leads to a desire for greater understanding. Nehemiah's calling stems from both a broken heart and an informed mind, for purpose needs both passion and knowledge.

Though he was not aware of God's purpose for him, Moses prepared to liberate the Israelites by learning in the court of Pharoah and being 'educated in all the wisdom of the Egyptians,'" and then later how to survive long periods in the desert during his exile in

* Wilkerson, p14.
** Acts 7:22.

Midian. The prophet Elisha prepared for his purpose by watching and learning from his mentor and predecessor, Elijah. We know almost nothing of how Jesus prepared for his ministry. Up until his baptism and forty days fasting in the wilderness, we have only one story about Jesus between his birth and the beginning of his ministry aged thirty, and it is of him aged twelve, in the temple in Jerusalem, sitting among the teachers, listening to them and asking them questions, and they were amazed at his understanding.*

In 1983, Bryan Stevenson, a nervous, naïve 23-year-old student at Harvard Law School, made his first visit to death row. He was doing an internship and had been told to visit a man called Henry to tell him that he would not be executed that year. The experience of meeting Henry on death row changed his life, giving him a new passion for justice, which led to a desire for a greater understanding.

> I went back to law school with an intense desire to understand the laws and doctrines that sanctioned the death penalty and extreme punishments. I piled up courses on constitutional law, litigation, appellate procedure, federal courts, and collateral remedies. I did extra work to broaden my understanding of how constitutional theory shapes criminal procedure. I plunged deeply into the law and the sociology of race, poverty, and power.**

Bryan Stevenson's passion translated into knowledge. I know that this can feel like a struggle, for we are often drawn to what is shallow over what is deep, celebrity news over the real news, and that our minds always prefer what is superficial over what is significant. But if we want to transform society, if we want to change the world, we need to become experts in the things that we're passionate about. Nehemiah's purpose develops because he studies and questions and is willing to look deeply at the real issues in the world.

* Luke 2:41–52.
** Bryan Stevenson, *Just Mercy: a Story of Justice and Redemption* (Scribe UK, 2015), p12.

COMMUNITY

Nehemiah would never have found this new passion or new understanding if it hadn't been for the people who came to see him. For Nehemiah's calling begins with community. It starts with a conversation: 'One of my brothers came ... with some other men, and I questioned them' (1:2). Later he gathers a group in Jerusalem, saying to them, 'You see the trouble we are in: Jerusalem lies in ruins, and its gates have been burned with fire. Come, let us rebuild the wall of Jerusalem, and we will no longer be in disgrace.' And they reply, 'Let us start rebuilding' (2:17–18).

It is in conversation that his heart is broken and his life is redirected; it is through community that he works out his great life purpose. For purpose is deeply personal but also essentially communal. It is personal in that God has something unique for each of us, but it is also communal in that our purpose is shaped by those around us.

Interestingly, it looks like Nehemiah knew only one of these people before the great turnaround of his life. When we welcome new people into our lives we are enriched, our perspective is expanded and our purpose emerges.

This has been one of the great joys of our calling to Rio de Janeiro. For through this process of moving across to the other side of the world, new people have come into our lives, who have helped us discern God's voice, given us encouragement and direction and who are now working alongside us as we try to live out this calling here.

PRAYER

But before we do anything we need to pray.

When we first arrived in Rio, we didn't know what we were supposed to do here. We knew that we were supposed to be in this city, and at Christ Church, but the exact nature of our ministry here was unclear. However, we knew we were supposed to pray. And for those first few months that was all we really did. We would gather each morning to pray in the church, then we had a week of prayer, and then a night of prayer, and then developed a rhythm of prayer three or four times a day. And it was out of these times that our purpose here began to take shape, and slowly it became clearer what we were supposed to be doing here.

Our calling is often revealed as we pray. Nehemiah writes, 'For some days I mourned and fasted and prayed before the God of heaven' (1:4). Prayer is the birthplace of our purpose because prayer is connection to God and God is the one from whom our purpose derives. If we are connected to God, he will always be speaking to us about our purpose. Prayer is the womb in which purpose grows and takes shape, where direction is clarified and a plan develops.

Before he tries to do anything, or make any plans, Nehemiah prays. One of the striking characteristics of Nehemiah is his practicality. He is good with plans and projects, highly organized and effective at getting things done. However, before he does anything, he prays. And after this time of prayer, he has total clarity on his plan of action. He knows exactly what to do, and what he will need to do it, so when the king asks him why he is so sad (2:2) he knows what to say and what to ask for (2:5–8).

We see something similar in the life of Jesus. After his baptism in the Jordan, in which God confirms his identity as his beloved son, he spends forty days in the desert, fasting and praying. He comes out of the desert to begin his ministry with a clear sense of his mission and the message he wants to give. Then, once his ministry has begun and life is becoming busy, he gets up early in the morning to pray, away from everyone else. When his disciples find him, he has a clear sense of what he should be doing next. After the feeding of the 5000, the well-fed crowd try to make him king, putting pressure on him to take his ministry in a direction that is not right, so again he withdraws to align himself with his purpose once more. Then, just before his arrest and execution, he goes to the garden at Gethsemane 'as usual' to pray, setting himself again to fulfil his purpose.*

Nehemiah's prayer is characterized by three features, each of which are important in the emergence of our calling: praise, repentance and submission. He praises God as 'the LORD, the God of heaven, the great and awesome God' (1:5). When we praise God, we acknowledge that God is the Lord of history, the one in control of all things, whose perspective is greater, whose plans are perfect, and therefore life is not an accident and our lives are not meaningless. He then repents, confessing the sins of his people, recognizing their rebellion against God (1:6–7). Repentance acknowledges that we have not lived out our calling, that we have gone our own way and lived according to our own desires instead of God's desires for us. Asking for repentance for the past opens the way for the future.

He finishes by addressing himself as God's 'servant', submitting himself to God's will and purposes (1:11). In prayers of submission, we place ourselves into God's hands. Just as Jesus prayed immediately before his arrest, 'Not my will, but yours be done,'** we align ourselves with God and his purposes for us, giving up our desires, our ambitions, our need for comfort, affirmation or security, so that we can embrace the purpose that God has for us.

Nehemiah asks not only to leave his role serving the king to travel to Jerusalem, but also for letters of approval and for access to resources to rebuild a city which had a long history of rebelling against the empires which tried to rule it. Back in the time of Ezra,*** this same king had commanded the building of the wall to stop, seeing any attempt to rebuild Jerusalem as a rebellion against him. But against all expectations, the king grants him everything he asks for. He is willing to lose a key adviser in Nehemiah and give him all resources and authority that he needs to fulfil his purpose.

What caused this change of heart for the king? The king changed

* Luke 4:1–15; Mark 1:35–38; John 6:15; Luke 22:39–46.
** Luke 22:42.
*** Ezra 4:17–23.

his mind because Nehemiah had been praying. He had been praying for a long time. Nehemiah started praying in the month of Kislev and he makes his request to the king in the month of Nisan. Between Kislev and Nisan are the months of Tevet, Shevat and Adar. So, he has been praying and fasting for around four months. This is what gives Nehemiah power to understand and fulfil his purpose. Nehemiah's prayers over the course of four months have brought human authorities and resources under divine control.

OPPOSITION

As our purpose becomes clear, so does opposition. As we step into God's calling, there will inevitably be new challenges, new problems and new struggles. Sometimes it is internal opposition, as we fight against our own selfishness or pride or apathy; often there can be external opposition, as we are confronted by people or institutions who resist our attempts to bring about change; and there is always spiritual opposition.

Nehemiah experiences very real opposition as soon as he begins his work, as Sanballat, Tobiah and Geshem mock, ridicule and spread false rumours about the returning Israelites (2:19). From the start there are enemies, objections and attacks.

There is always opposition to the purposes of God for our lives. The people of Israel always had to deal with opposition. The psalmists frequently write about struggles with enemies and opponents. A significant proportion of the Gospels relate to Jesus dealing with different forms of opposition. And throughout the Acts of the Apostles the disciples face attempts by the authorities to crush the growth of the church. This can be painful and discouraging, but it can also be a sign that we are following the call of God. As God's purposes are always opposed, the very presence of opposition can be a helpful sign that we are on the right path.

In our first few months in Brazil there seemed to be so much opposition. It felt exhausting, discouraging and a massive distraction from what we felt we should be doing. But we held on to the encouragement that the opposition we faced was a sign that we were on the right path.

What we see as obstacles to our purpose may reinforce our calling. Opposition can increase our passion, deepen our knowledge, strengthen community and fuel our prayers. The opposition we encountered in Brazil included some of the toughest and most personal attacks I've ever experienced, but it also helped to clarify our purpose, motivating us to pray, galvanizing the team and strengthening the mission that God gave us to do.

In the end, the opposition we face is not an obstacle to the purposes of God being fulfilled. Very often it is how God's purposes are fulfilled. For it is in opposition that our character is formed, and our purpose is refined and ultimately carried out. Joseph endured years of opposition, but this only transformed his character from an immature teenager to a person with the maturity, wisdom and authority to rule Egypt. Pharoah's opposition to Moses led to the miraculous crossing of the Red Sea and a story which would define the identity of the people of Israel for hundreds of years. The young errand boy David experienced opposition in the form of a giant Philistine, but this only helped him become a great warrior. The prophet Elijah experienced opposition from King Ahab and Queen Jezebel, and it resulted in the confrontation and defeat of the prophets of Baal. Jesus experienced opposition throughout his life, and at its most intense it took him to the cross, but that brought about the fulfilment of his purpose in the salvation of the world.

The presence of opposition reminds us that calling, though often beautiful and exciting, can also be painful and frustrating. And next we will move from discovering our calling to look at the struggles and difficulties of following that calling.

PART THREE

Struggle

Chapter 12

BROKEN

Elijah
1 Kings 19

He came to a broom bush, sat under it and prayed that he might die. 'I have had enough, Lord,' he said. 'Take my life; I am no better than my ancestors.'

1 KINGS 19:4

And the word of the Lord came to him: 'What are you doing here, Elijah?'

1 KINGS 19:9

Moneypenny: [They say] that what you did in Mexico was one
step too far, that you're finished.
James Bond: And what do you think?
Moneypenny: I think you're just getting started.

SPECTRE*

And then, sometimes, everything seems to fall apart. Before we are called, after we have been called, as we are being called, something happens which shakes everything we thought we knew and could rely on, and we are left feeling devastated, confused, heartbroken and disappointed. Then we are confronted by this fundamental question: what are you doing here?

'What are you doing here, Elijah?' (1 Kings 19:9). This is the

---

* Sam Mendes, *Spectre* (Sony Pictures, 2015).

question with which God confronts Elijah at Mount Horeb. It is also the question that God asks us: What are you doing here? And there are essentially five possible answers we can give to this question, if we are being honest with ourselves.

First, we might be *running* from something. We are trying to escape, avoiding difficulty, responsibility and failure. Second, we might be *conforming*. We are doing what everyone else is doing, fitting in, going along with all the things that people would expect us to. Third, we might be *proving*, trying to impress, succeed, beat the competition, show the world that we are something rather than nothing. Fourth, we might be *drifting*. Life is something that happens to us, and we drift from relationship to relationship, job to job, activity to activity without much thought or intention. Or there is the fifth option, which is that we are living out God's call on our lives.

This question of 'What are you doing here?' often becomes clearest when life is toughest. For during these times, we are forced to reassess our lives and ask ourselves what we are really doing. As we have seen already, our purpose often emerges from our struggles and brokenness, from disappointment, failure and confusion.

Life is always difficult in some way. But there are periods when life is particularly difficult, and, in my experience, it is in these times of crisis that we find that our purpose is reshaped, refined and redirected. We find our purpose emerging not from ease, but from pain; not from success, but out of failure; not from the high points, but the lowest points.

This is what we see in the story of Elijah in 1 Kings 19. We do not have an account of Elijah's original call to be a prophet. He simply appears, serving God faithfully and powerfully. He has some great successes, confronting evil rulers, raising a child from the dead and then having a showdown with the prophets of Baal, in which fire falls from heaven, showing conclusively that Yahweh is the true God of

Israel.* But then everything falls apart, and he goes through a time of darkness and despair. Immediately after his greatest success, Elijah enters a deep emotional darkness, as he faces opposition, isolation, exhaustion and depression. The queen wants to kill him; he wants to die; he is alone and wants to give up (19:1–3).

We do not know the cause of this depression for certain, whether it was related to his family history or genetic factors, but we can see two possible reasons here. The first is burnout. It looks like his output has exceeded his input. This story starts with Elijah having a couple of meals which last him forty days (19:6–8), and this might be a picture of what has been happening for years: Elijah has been giving out more than he has been taking in, and he is depleted physically, emotionally and spiritually. He is drained and it feels like he has nothing left. Many of us can empathize with this – we can feel like we have been running on empty: weary, depleted, burning out.

The other cause of his depression could be trauma. He gets some bad news: the queen wants him dead and he knows that she usually gets her way. Sometimes a sudden disappointment or painful event can push us into a dark time. We go through a break-up, a rejection, a bereavement or lose our job and it plunges us into depression.

For Elijah it may have been a combination of these factors. Elijah has been battling a king who wanted to kill him for years, so it seems strange that this message affects him so severely now. But perhaps his exhaustion has made him more vulnerable than he had been before. The sustained stress means that what he was once able to cope with now shakes him and he feels broken.

In these painful times beautiful things can emerge. It was in the darkest times in Israel's history that their calling as the people of God took shape. It was in the desert, after escaping from slavery in Egypt, that they received the Ten Commandments and the Law, and Israel was formed into a nation. It was during the exile in Babylon,

* 1 Kings 17 – 18.

when they lost their land, their king, their temple and their freedom, that much of the Old Testament was written and collected, and new hopes emerged which would ultimately point to the coming of Jesus. And it was in their own personal struggles that David and others wrote the most beautiful, moving and profound songs, which we now have recorded in the Psalms. Isaiah writes,

I will give you the treasures of darkness
And hidden riches of secret places

ISAIAH 45:3 (NKJV)

Nassir Ghaemi, the professor of psychiatry at Tufts University School of Medicine in Boston, writes about how many of the greatest leaders in history struggled with mental illness: Mahatma Gandhi, Martin Luther King, Winston Churchill, John F Kennedy, Franklin D Roosevelt, Ted Turner, Abraham Lincoln. He argues that their mental illness, though a source of great pain, was also the key to their brilliance. For out of their depression and mania, valuable qualities emerged, particularly realism, creativity, empathy and resilience. He writes, 'Their weakness is, in short, the secret of their strength.'*

Elijah goes through this dark time, and through it he encounters God in a whole new way. New people are brought into his life, and he finds a new direction, a new plan, a new way of working. Through the brokenness, God calls him again. His purpose is renewed and redirected.

A NEW KIND OF LISTENING

In his moment of crisis Elijah goes to exactly the right place. He goes to 'the mountain of God', where God had appeared to Moses and spoken to him. Like Samuel, he was in the place where you hear from God. Our purpose does not reside within us, but within God.

* Nassir Ghaemi, *A First-Rate Madness: Uncovering the Links between Leadership and Mental Illness* (Penguin, 2011), p19.

God is the one with the purpose and when we are connected to him, we join in with his purpose. Your purpose is not primarily internal and individual. It is relational. It comes from a relationship with one whose purpose is perfect and who gives meaning to our lives. We discover our purpose by listening. And by *really* listening.

When God speaks to Elijah here, it is not through the wind, the earthquake or the fire (19:11–12). These would have forced Elijah to hear God's voice whether he wanted to or not. Instead, he speaks to him through a gentle whisper, which meant Elijah had to stand still and really listen. So he went and stood at the edge of his cave, put his cloak over his head to avoid any distractions and listened properly (19:13).

In the toughest times we are forced to really listen to God. For me, I know that there are two ways that I listen to people. I can be getting on with things, washing up, writing emails, but also listening to what is going on around me. I am listening, but my attention is divided. Or I can be really listening, focusing completely on the person who is in front of me.

It can be the same with God. We can be vaguely listening as we get on with the rest of life, trying to be open to his voice, but with our attention also on daily life, the news, the people around us. Or we can be totally focused, with our full attention on God.

When Timothy Keller first planted Redeemer Presbyterian Church in New York, he told his wife Kathy that he knew the first three years were going to be tough and would involve lots of long hours, but that after that he would be more available to her and the children. After three years Kathy reminded him of what they had agreed and asked him to cut back his hours, but he told her it would need just a few more months. The months went by but still no change took place.

One day he came home to find the door to the balcony was open and he heard a smashing noise as he came in. And then another smash. He walked onto the balcony and found Kathy sitting on the floor with a hammer and next to her a stack of their wedding china and on the ground the remains of two saucers.

'What are you doing?' he asked her.

She looked up at him and said, 'You're not listening to me. You don't realize that if you keep working these hours you are going to destroy this family. I don't know how to get through to you. You aren't seeing how serious this is. This is what you are doing.' And she smashed the next saucer with her hammer.

He sat down quickly. 'I'm listening. I'm listening', he said. And he really listened. The arguments were the same as they had always been, but they finally cut through his delusions. He said that he was addicted to productivity and there would be no convenient time to cut back. He had to do something now. She saw that he was really listening for the first time, and they hugged and were reconciled.

He then said, 'When I heard the smashing, I thought you were having a breakdown.' Then she smiled and said, 'Do you see those three saucers I smashed?' We don't have any cups for them. They broke years ago. They were spare saucers. But I'm glad you sat down before I had to break any more!'*

Sometimes God allows things to break in us so that we might finally really listen, enabling us to hear his voice in new ways, through silence and stillness. And through listening we rediscover our purpose.

A NEW WAY OF OPERATING

One of the features of this passage is Elijah's loneliness. He has become locked into himself. When God asks him what he's doing, he says, 'I have been zealous ... I am the only one left' (19:10). He has become self-consumed, focusing in on himself and feeling like everyone else has compromised. He has lost perspective. It's not true that he is the only one left. There's his servant whom he chose to

* Tim Keller, *The Meaning of Marriage: Facing the Complexities of Commitment with the Wisdom of God* (Hodder & Stoughton, 2011), p146.

leave behind (19:3). He also seems to have forgotten about Obadiah, another follower of the Lord, whom he met before his breakdown (18:7).

Partly, this reflects the isolating nature of pain. One of the problems of suffering is that it is so individual. No one can understand completely what we are feeling and so it naturally isolates us. We feel more vulnerable. Other people have the capacity to hurt us unwittingly so it feels safer to be alone. But it also highlights how Elijah has been living up till now. He has done some extraordinary things, but he has been acting alone. He has been operating independently and he has become self-occupied.

But now God reshapes his purpose, tuning his ear to really listen, making him stand still in his presence, reconnecting Elijah to God again. Then he reconnects Elijah to other people. He says, 'Anoint Hazael ... anoint Jehu ... anoint Elisha' (19:15–16). Elijah has been talking to God about himself, but God talks to him about other people. Elijah has been working alone, achieving great things alone, but his task now is to help three others to discover and fulfil their purposes.

These three figures are new names in the story. It is time for new people to come into his life. If he is going to fulfil God's purpose, he will need other people. God is saying to him that it is now time to work with and through others. Before, he was working alone; from now on he will work with Elisha. Before, he acted independently; now he is to work through collaboration and community. God reminds him that he is not as alone as he thinks he is, for there are 'seven thousand' others who are faithfully following the Lord (19:18).

He is told to go to new people and to new places ('the desert of Damascus'). This is not the end. It is just the beginning. God says to Elijah, 'Go back the way you came' (19:15). Elijah thought, and perhaps wished, that it was the end for him. But God says to him, 'Go back.' It's not over. You might think you're finished; but you're only just getting started.

Peter Scazzero, in his book *Emotionally Healthy Spirituality*, describes six stages of spiritual growth. The first three stages are a 'Life-Changing Awareness of God', 'Discipleship', and 'The Active Life'. However, at some point we all hit 'The Wall'. This refers to a crisis point, where something significant goes wrong in our life. It is more than the daily struggles and frustrations of life, which characterize life for all people. It is an event or an experience which shakes us to our core: a major illness, a bereavement, a breakup, a moral failure. It challenges everything we thought we knew about God, ourselves and the world.

At this point we have three options. We can bounce out, deciding to abandon our faith because it no longer works for us. We thought that being a Christian would make life easier but, if anything, it seems to be making life harder and so we opt out. We can try to bounce back, attempting to return to how life was before by ignoring what has taken place and refusing to process the pain of what has happened. Alternatively, we can go through 'The Wall' to the 'Journey Inward', beginning to see ourselves in a new light, face some uncomfortable truths about ourselves and recognize our own pride, selfishness and lack of understanding.

From here we can enter the next stage, the 'Journey Outward', in which we start to serve God and others again, but out of a new humility, compassion and empathy. Finally, we reach the stage 'Transformed into Love', as God's love invades every part of our lives and we begin to love God whether things go well or badly, whether we can understand what is happening or life feels confusing. Much like the marriage vows, we say to God, 'for better, for worse, for richer, for poorer, in sickness and in health: no matter what happens, I will love you'. This in turn enables us to experience God in a new way, restarting the whole process.[*]

Elijah seems to be going through something like this process. He has gone through 'The Wall', he has encountered God in a new way

---

[*] Peter Scazzero, *Emotionally Healthy Spirituality: It's Impossible to be Spiritually Mature while Remaining Emotionally Immature* (Zondervan, 2017), pp119–120.

and his purpose has been renewed. In these times of disappointment, exhaustion and depression, the temptation is to give up. It can feel like we are finished. But then we discover that God is telling us that we are only just getting started.

Jesus himself went through the darkest time of despair, but through it he achieved his purpose. He prayed that he might be able to avoid it, but, ultimately, he knew he had to go through it to fulfil what God had called him to do. And the other side of the cross was the resurrection, a new start, a new hope, a new creation. Out of his brokenness came renewal for the world, and out of our brokenness a new purpose can emerge.

Chapter 13

SILENCE

Esther

Esther 4

---

*Do not think that because you are in the king's house you alone
of all the Jews will escape. For if you remain silent at this time,
relief and deliverance for the Jews will arise from another place,
but you and your father's family will perish. And who knows but
that you have come to your royal position for such a time as this?*

ESTHER 4:13−14

It's all wrong. By rights we shouldn't even be here. But we are. It's
like in the great stories, Mr Frodo. The ones that really mattered.
Full of darkness and danger they were. And sometimes you
didn't want to know the end. Because how could the end be
happy. How could the world go back to the way it was when so
much bad had happened. But in the end, it's only a passing thing,
this shadow. Even darkness must pass. A new day will come. And
when the sun shines it will shine out the clearer. Those were the
stories that stayed with you. That meant something. Even if you
were too small to understand why.

THE LORD OF THE RINGS: THE TWO TOWERS*

Between our return from Hong Kong in June 2020 and the first
thought of Brazil in June 2021, I felt directionless. There had been
plenty of themes which God seemed to highlight for me in Hong

---

* Peter Jackson, *The Lord of the Rings: The Two Towers* (New Line Cinema, 2002).

Kong, and then there had been a strong feeling that we were not supposed to be in Brighton when we first got back. But after that there was nothing. There was no clear sign to show us what to do next. At the same time everything around us was changing rapidly, with many people in pain, confused and finding life difficult.

The book of Esther is the story of a young Jewish girl facing a terrible situation. Set during the period of the exile, when her people have lost their homeland and become a minority in a foreign empire, she goes through a degrading and traumatic process by which she is selected as the new queen of Persia. Then she gets news that there is a plan for the total destruction of her own people by the second most powerful person in the empire, and even though she is queen, she lacks any power to make a difference. In the middle of this personal and national crisis, God is silent. In fact, he is not mentioned once in the whole book of Esther.

Until now the stories of calling we've looked at have had at least some degree of clarity. For Adam and Eve, for Abraham, Joseph, Moses, Gideon and Elijah, God speaks clearly through a voice, a burning bush, a dream, an angel, through signs or at least a gentle whisper. There may be doubts, confusion or reluctance, but clearly God is doing or saying something. For Ruth, David and Nehemiah, their sense of calling comes from a deep inner conviction. They may not hear an external voice or receive a divine visitation, but they are totally clear about what they are supposed to do. But now we come to a story marked both by God's silence and an uncertainty about what to do.

Esther will eventually act with extraordinary courage and conviction, but not because she has heard God's voice or knows with any clarity what she should do. Her cousin, Mordecai, on hearing of the plans to annihilate all the Jews, sends a message to her, asking her to help, and saying, 'Who knows but that you have come to your royal position for such a time as this' (4:14). It is a statement of uncertainty: 'Who knows …?' At similar crisis moments in its national life, other figures from Israel's history had clear directions from God – Esther has not received any of these. In fact, God himself appears to be totally hidden. He is at work, but invisibly. And yet this silence and uncertainty does not stop Esther moving into action and fulfilling the purpose that God has for her.

It is easy to feel paralysed by uncertainty. But Esther's story shows us what to do when God is silent and we are uncertain about what we are supposed to be doing. The silence and uncertainty should not prevent us from acting. Nor does a lack of clarity mean that we are not called.

ASSUMING YOU ARE IN THE RIGHT PLACE

First, we can assume that we are where we are for a purpose. Mordecai persuades Esther that maybe she is exactly where she needs to be to do what God is asking her to do, and that she has come to her position as queen for a purpose.

It is easy to feel like we should be somewhere else: another country, another job, living at another time. Esther had several reasons for thinking she shouldn't be in this position. For a start, she wasn't supposed to be in Persia. She was supposed to be in Israel; it was only the sins of her ancestors, and the territorial ambitions of first the Babylonian and then the Persian empires, which had brought her to the city of Susa. She really shouldn't have been married to the king, who had only divorced his previous wife because she had embarrassed him at a party. The king had chosen Esther, not after a period of courting in which they had gone for a few fun dates, discovered they had mutual interests, mutual respect, similar values and a joint calling, but after a horrific and oppressive process which ended with the king choosing her because he 'was attracted to Esther more than to any of the other women' (2:17). This was not a position that she had chosen for herself, nor had it come from any deep desire or sense of calling within her. Her cousin Mordecai had talked her into applying for the role in the first place. And she had only succeeded by concealing her race. Esther could have justifiably thought to herself, 'I should not be here; I should not be in this position.'

Many of the stories of calling involve a change of location. God calls Abram to leave Ur and go to Canaan. He calls Moses to leave Midian and go to Egypt, Ruth to leave Moab and go to Israel and Nehemiah to leave Persia and return to Jerusalem. But until God directs us elsewhere, we should assume that we are where we are for a purpose. Paul will later write, 'Each person should remain in the situation they were in when God called them.'* Even if our position feels like it is the result of injustice, mistakes or accidents (as it may have done for Esther), we can believe that God has brought us to where we are for a reason. We might feel like we have none of the right skills to deal with the situations with which we are faced, but unless God calls us elsewhere it is best to assume that we are in exactly the right place for the work that God has for us to do.

ASSUMING THAT THIS IS THE RIGHT TIME

Mordecai says to Esther that maybe she's in this position for this particular time. He's trying to persuade her that it is the right time to act. Patience is a vital part of the Christian life. It is the first quality that Paul uses to describe love,** and it was the central virtue of the early church.*** However, patience is not procrastination. There is always a danger that we delay doing what is right, never feeling like it is quite the right time. When I visited Jackie Pullinger's organization aged nineteen, staying there for a few weeks, I remember thinking that this kind of life was amazing, beautiful and exactly how I was supposed to live, but it was too difficult. However, I considered that if I was married, then I would do this kind of work. I would have the support and comfort of marriage, and that would enable me to give up so

---

* 1 Corinthians 7:20.
** 1 Corinthians 13:4.
*** Alan Kreider, *The Patient Ferment of the Early Church: The Improbable Rise of Christianity in the Roman Empire* (Baker Academic, 2016), p1.

much and live among those who were finding freedom from heroin addiction in Hong Kong. Then after I got married, I started thinking about this kind of work again, and thought to myself, I would love to live this kind of life, but I can't because I'm married. It wouldn't be fair on Tara and the children. But if I was single, then I could. I would be more flexible, have more time, and could really throw myself into this kind of work. It's never a convenient time. It's always difficult to make a radical change.

In his short story, *A Talk Among Leisured People*, Leo Tolstoy describes a wealthy dinner party in Russia consisting of several different generations, talking about the need to give up their lifestyles and go to live among the poor. A student who is there announces that he is going to do this, but his father reminds him that it would be better for him to finish his studies, and then he will have more to offer. A middle-aged married man then says that he will go, but his wife reminds him of his duty to her and to their family, and that he should wait until the children are older. Finally, an old man tells the group that he will go, but the others remind him that at his age the change could be too much for him. Each member of that group is persuaded that it is not yet the time to act, that at some future point it would be easier or more beneficial, and so no one does anything except continue in their current lifestyle. A visitor observing the conversation concludes, 'So it seems that none of us may live rightly: we may only talk about it.'

Martin Luther King Jr wrote from Birmingham Jail in Alabama, 'For years now I have heard the word "Wait!" ... This "Wait" has almost always meant "Never." We must come to see, with one of our distinguished jurists, that "justice too long delayed is justice denied."'**

Maybe you're in the position you're in for this time, to act now.

---

* Leo Tolstoy, *Walk in the Light and Twenty-Three Tales*, tr. Louise and Aylmer Maude (Orbis Books, 2003), pp3–7.
** Martin Luther King Jr, *Letter from Birmingham Jail*, April 16, 1963, africa.upenn.edu (accessed May 2024).

CONNECTING WITH THE PROBLEMS AROUND YOU

If we are in the right place at the right time, then we can assume that the problems around us are for us to engage with. This is not my instinct. My initial response to the social or cultural issues around me is to hide and withdraw. It is all too painful and too complicated. I cannot process all the opinions and emotions which are now broadcast so quickly across all platforms. And so, my instinct is to retreat into my own world, and to distract myself with sports news or history podcasts, instead of engaging with what is happening.

When Mordecai says to Esther, 'Do not think that because you are in the king's house you alone of all the Jews will escape' (4:13), he is saying to her 'this is your issue too.' It can be easy to think, 'this has nothing to do with me' or 'at least this won't affect us.' Esther might have reasoned, 'No one knows I'm a Jew. I'm married to the king. I'll be OK.' But Mordecai reminds her that this is her problem too. We are called to connect to the problems we see in the world, to see them as our problems, even if they don't affect us directly.

This is a common element of these stories of calling we've looked at. God persuades Moses to connect to the suffering of the Hebrew slaves in Egypt, Gideon that ending the oppression from the Midianites is an issue in which he can play a part, and Nehemiah that the state of Jerusalem, though miles away, is something for him to direct his life towards.

And so we must ask ourselves: is there something happening in my life, in my family or my city, an issue or an injustice, which I have been assuming has nothing to do with me but that God wants to become my problem too?

OPERATING IN NEW WAYS

When we begin to assume that we are in the right place and the right time, when we begin to connect to the problems around us,

God responds by drawing out of us qualities and characteristics which had not previously emerged. As Esther connects to the terrible violence which is about to happen, we see aspects of her character which had not appeared earlier in the story. Up until this point Esther has operated by concealing her identity, by doing as she has been told, and being directed by the men in her life, her cousin Mordecai, the eunuch Hegai who was in charge of the harem, and the king. She has gone along with the systems already in place, skilfully navigating the ways the court works, without disrupting anything or upsetting anyone along the way. And she is known for her beauty, modesty and charm.

But now, once Mordecai has challenged her and helped her see the responsibility arising out of her uniquely privileged position, we see a change. The injustice she sees, the compassion she feels and the actions she begins to make transform her. She moves from being passive to being active. She directs Mordecai to get everyone praying (4:16). She takes a huge risk and defies convention by approaching the king without having been summoned (5:1). She organizes a banquet. She confronts Haman, the second most powerful man in the empire, with the strongest language (7:6). She has gone from concealing her race to revealing her race. She has moved from going along with the system to defying the system, and instead of being led by the men around her, she now takes the lead, instructing, confronting and challenging them.

When we are faced with new and difficult circumstances, it requires different ways of working and operating, leaving behind old patterns and assumptions so that we can take up new ways of working. There will be qualities deep within us, which we had no idea were there, but which God intends to bring to the surface for this time and for his purposes.

God even enables us to make sacrifices which we never thought we would be capable of making. Esther knows that doing what she is called to do will mean risking what she has. She wants to save her people, but she cannot do this without personal risk, even the risk of death. But she is willing to give up the position she has as queen, the lifestyle she enjoys in the palace, the privileges she has become accustomed to, and even her life, so that she can fulfil the role which God has prepared for her.

This is how Esther saved her people, and it is how Jesus saved the world. He gave up his position, gave up heaven, gave up his life to save us. This then becomes the model for our lives. We love each other by laying down our lives for one another. There is no way to confront injustice, live compassionately or fulfil God's purpose for us without laying down our lives in some way. As Jackie Pullinger put it, 'The principle of the gospel is this: the gospel always brings life to the one who receives it, and death to the one who brings it.'*

Esther does all this whilst not knowing for sure. She risks her life even in the uncertainty. She acts with total courage, despite not hearing God's voice or being reassured of his presence.

SUPPLIED WITH NEW RESOURCES

In addition to the inner transformation which enables us to do what we need to do, God also provides us with the external resources to fulfil our calling.

Against all odds, Esther succeeds in her plans. Haman is exposed and removed. Mordecai is honoured. The king is supportive. But the edict condemning the Jews cannot be removed. The threat remains. However, Xerxes issues another edict which gives the Jewish people the right to defend themselves (8:11).

This is a picture of how God often seems to work. Of course God can, and sometimes does, remove the challenges we face – illnesses, stresses, annoying people – but more often, he seems to give us what we need to face these challenges and to overcome them. Therefore,

* St Stephen's Society: the official website of Jackie Pullinger, ststephenssociety.com (accessed May 2024).

we pray for healing, and we pray for peace, believing that God acts to remove what needs to be removed. But we also pray that God will equip us and strengthen us, to give us everything we need to fight those things which he has not yet removed: injustice, poverty, loneliness and lostness.

Our purpose can emerge even in the silence. We ask God to speak, seeking his guidance and giving him every opportunity to speak to us, being willing to do whatever God asks us to do. Very often we will not be told explicitly what to do, but that does not mean we are operating outside of God's purposes. Raniero Cantalamessa puts it like this, 'I have submitted the question to God, I have emptied myself of my own will. I have renounced deciding for myself and I have given God the chance to intervene in my life if he so wishes. Whatever I decide to do, based on the ordinary criteria of judgement, will be obedience to God.'*

We might ask God to remove the uncertainty, and often he will respond by speaking to us through the Bible and the people around us or through inner conviction. But often, instead of removing the uncertainty, he gives us what we need to live obediently and faithfully in the middle of the uncertainty. Life will never be totally secure, nor our calling totally clear. For he alone is the certain one. He alone is our rock, the eternal one and the solid ground on which we stand. Everything else might be uncertain, but we have with us, and in us, the one who certainly loves us, and certainly directs us, and certainly works through us in extraordinary ways.

* Raniero Cantalamessa, *Obedience* (St Pauls, 1989), p56.

Chapter 14

PAIN

Isaiah
Isaiah 6

In the year that King Uzziah died, I saw the Lord, high and exalted, seated on a throne; and the train of his robe filled the temple.

ISAIAH 6:1

If it falls your lot to be a street sweeper, sweep streets like Raphael painted pictures; sweep streets like Michelangelo carved marble; sweep streets like Beethoven composed music; sweep streets like Shakespeare wrote poetry; sweep streets so well that all the host of heaven and earth will have to pause and say: 'Here lived a great street sweeper who swept his job well.'

MARTIN LUTHER KING JR*

Sometimes God calls us to continue what we are already doing, but in a whole new way. Isaiah was a prophet, speaking on behalf of God to his people over many years during the reign of some of Judah's last kings before they were conquered by the Babylonians. In the sixth chapter of his prophetic book, we read an account of God appearing to Isaiah and calling him. However, this does not mark the start of his prophetic ministry. He has already been a prophet

---

*Martin Luther King Jr, "Some Things We Must Do," Address Delivered at the Second Annual Institute on Nonviolence and Social Change at Holt Street Baptist Church, 5 December 1957, kinginstitute.stanford.edu (accessed June 2024).

for some time. He has already been speaking on behalf of God to his people, giving God's perspective on history and on their lives. Until now Isaiah has been a prophet, and then God appears to him and calls him to continue to be a prophet.

In the Bible, and in church history, there are many stories of God calling people to something new, sending them to new places or commanding them to adopt new roles. God calls Abram to move to a new country; God calls David to do a new role in the same place. Sometimes God calls people to change both place and role, as he does when he sends Moses back to Egypt to become a liberator instead of a shepherd. The call of God often involves a significant change, whether of place or of role. However, here we have something different but equally important: God's calling to do what we were already doing in the place we've been doing it, but in a whole new way.

You might be a teacher, and then God calls you to be a teacher. You might be a student, and then God calls you to study. You might be a father or mother, and then God calls you to be a parent. You will be doing the same role in the same place, but God infuses your work, your location and your relationships with greater meaning and significance than they had before. There is a world of difference between living in Brighton because you were born there, or because you like living by the sea, and being called to Brighton because you know that this is where God wants you to be. And there is a world of difference between having a job to earn money or for the enjoyment of the work, and engaging in that work out of obedience to God to serve him through that work. We can be married or single because we want to be in a relationship or want to be single, but it is quite another matter to be called to either marriage or singleness for the sake of the kingdom of God.

Sometimes God calls us to a whole new life stage, new relationships, a new place, a new life's work, and sometimes God enters our current life stage, our location and our work to give us greater purpose in them.

But it is not always an easy process. Isaiah's new sense of purpose does not emerge from a new-found inner strength, or a great success, or from being given additional resources. It emerges instead from pain, and an awareness of his weakness, from loss and grief. It is out of his vulnerability that God calls and sends Isaiah. It is out of our loss and grief that God works to reveal or renew our calling.

TURNING OUR PAIN INTO PURPOSE

Isaiah's call emerges out of pain. It begins in the context of grief, for Isaiah relates that his encounter with God took place 'in the year that King Uzziah died' (6:1). Uzziah had reigned in Judah for fifty-two years, doing 'what was right in the eyes of the LORD',* and the nation had experienced relative security and prosperity.** But now he had died, and at the same time Tiglath-Pileser III had come to power in Assyria, the greatest empire of the time, and was looking to expand. The small state of Judah on his border was looking vulnerable. It was a time of grief for what they had lost and uncertainty about the future.

As Isaiah faces the loss of their king in Judah and the rise of another, hostile, king, he has a vision of God. And it is a vision of God as 'the King, the LORD Almighty' (6:5), sitting on his throne, with his train filling the temple. Here is the King, not just of Judah, but of the whole world. The king of Judah may be dead, and there may be a foreign king of a powerful empire threatening them, but on the throne is the universal King, who is more powerful than any

---

* 2 Kings 15:3.

** Uzziah was not without his faults. Though both 2 Kings and 2 Chronicles insist that he did what was right in the eyes of the Lord, they acknowledge that he failed to remove the high places, and the great successes he had during his reign caused him to become proud, burning incense on the altar though not a priest, and as a result ended his life with leprosy, living separately and handing responsibility for the kingdom to his son Jothan.

kingdom or empire in the world.

The experience of pain often enables us to experience God in new ways. When we are struggling financially, we get to experience God as provider. When we are vulnerable, we experience God as our rock and refuge. When we are lost, we experience God as our guide. When we have four young children, we get to experience the God who is true rest for our souls. When someone we love dies, we get to experience God as the resurrection and the life. As we go through pain, God reveals himself to us in new ways.

Isaiah sees God in a new way through the pain of loss. And this begins to shape a key theme in Isaiah's message to the nations, of God as the universal King, sovereign over all things, over the rise and fall of all nations, in control even when we cannot see it, and whose purposes are beyond anything that we could understand.

His purpose emerges from his pain. We see this often: those who have had painful family experiences now working to strengthen families, those who were homeless helping people who are still on the streets, those who struggled with addictions helping others find freedom. God reveals himself in our pain, then gives us something beautiful and valuable to share out of our pain. So instead of running from the pain and disappointments, we can allow God to touch them, reveal himself in them and create purpose out of them.

BECOMING SMALLER TO MAKE OUR PURPOSE BIGGER

When Isaiah sees this vision of God as King, he cries out, 'I am ruined' (6:5). He literally says, 'I am silenced.' The prophet whose job it is to speak is silenced. Suddenly he can't do the very thing he feels he should be doing. Sometimes God needs to silence us before he can work through our words. Sometimes God needs to stop us to get us moving in the right direction. Sometimes God allows us to fall apart so that he can put us back together. Sometimes God needs to make us smaller to fulfil a bigger purpose in our lives. Hundreds of years later Jesus would fulfil his purpose by making himself smaller, the omnipresent and omnipotent God, coming to earth as a tiny baby, adopting human weakness and frailty, so that he could save the world.

For Isaiah, the purpose of his life will emerge from a combination of an enlarged view of God and a reduced view of himself. As he sees the holiness of God, Isaiah suddenly becomes more aware of his sin. It is a difficult experience for Isaiah, as it always is whenever we are confronted by the reality of our sins.

There are different kinds of weakness, and different ways that we respond to them. There are physical weaknesses, which for me would include a tendency to fatigue, a back which aches if I stand still for too long, an inability to touch my toes and a misshapen big toe on my right foot. Then there are emotional weaknesses, like my acute sensitivity, my tendency to cry when watching or hearing almost anything vaguely emotional and my capacity to feel down for no good reason. There are also mental weaknesses, like my tendency to lose things, my difficulty with spelling or remembering certain types of information and my slow processing when listening. But then beneath and more fundamental than all these other kinds of weakness, there are our spiritual weaknesses, which the Bible calls 'sin', and which would include our pride, selfishness, lust, jealousy, prejudice, selfish ambition, control and passivity.

The first three kinds of weaknesses are often embarrassing, but they are much easier to talk about than our spiritual weaknesses. Our sin is harder to see in ourselves, harder to admit to others, far more damaging in its consequences and therefore much more important to address. For the primary problem in the world is not physical, emotional or mental, but spiritual.

For God to fulfil his purposes in us and through us, we must recognize our weaknesses, for what is unseen and unacknowledged is most dangerous. Isaiah must know that he is a sinner before he can take up his calling. This awareness is both personal and universal (6:5). He understands his personal sin ('I am a man of unclean lips') and the universality of sin ('and I live among a people of unclean lips'). Both are necessary: it is not enough to be aware of general sin, the faults and weaknesses of others, but be blind to our own. Nor is it helpful to think that we are the only ones who struggle and have failed in the ways that we do.

Each time I have sensed a dramatic call to something new, to Brighton in 2009 and to Brazil in 2021, it has been preceded by a time of feeling particularly weak, being forced to address my own sins and inadequacies. I had to become smaller to be ready for what God had prepared for me.

It is essential that we are aware of our weaknesses precisely in the areas to which we are called. Isaiah says, 'I am a man of unclean lips' (6:5). He becomes aware of his sinful words, the sinful way he speaks, so that he can fulfil his purpose as a prophet.

If we are called into the world of politics, we need to be aware of our ambition. If we are called into the world of finances, we need to be aware of our greed. If we are called to leadership, we need to be aware of our desire for power and control. If we are called into the caring professions, we need to be aware of our hard-heartedness. If we are called to marriage and family life, we need to be aware of our own selfishness.

Once we are aware of our weaknesses and inadequacies, it is easier for God to work through us for his purposes. In *Prince Caspian*, Aslan meets with Caspian, who is called to be the new king of Narnia, and asks him,

'Do you feel yourself sufficient to take up the Kingship of Narnia?'

'I – I don't think I do, Sir,' said Caspian. 'I'm only a kid.'

'Good,' said Aslan. 'If you had felt yourself sufficient, it would have been a proof that you were not.'*

God makes us smaller, and this enables us to become part of something greater.

* CS Lewis, *Prince Caspian* (HarperCollins Children's Books, 2023), pp217–218.

WORKING IN US TO WORK THROUGH US

God is calling Isaiah to be a prophet, and therefore to speak. Isaiah's message will be one which both confronts the people of Judah with their injustice, pride, social inequality and the neglect of the poor, but also promises reconciliation and restoration in the future. However, before Isaiah can carry this message, he needs both to recognize his own sin and also experience forgiveness and reconciliation for himself. And so, God sends a piece of coal, touching Isaiah's mouth with it, and saying, 'See, this has touched your lips; your guilt is taken away and your sin atoned for' (6:7).

If we want to bring about social transformation, we need to experience personal transformation. If we want to bring freedom to others, we need to allow God to set us free. Deep internal work is what enables a powerful external work. We need to receive from God so that we can give something to others. God wants to work through you. He has a purpose for you. But to work through you he first needs to work in you.

One of the dangers of the Christian life consists of being totally focused on helping others, offering guidance or showing kindness, but not allowing God to do anything for you; wanting to change the world but not letting God change you. Another is being so totally focused on our own inner transformation that we forget to pass this on to anyone else, failing to remember that what God is doing for us is not just for us but for those to whom he sends us.

Our purpose emerges from what God has done and continues to do for us personally. Jackie Pullinger is one of the most extraordinary Christian leaders in the world today, working with the triad gang members and addicts of Hong Kong for over fifty years, and seeing the remarkable transformation of lives. She was once asked, 'What sustains you in your ministry?' and she replied, 'Jesus died for me. What more do I need?' She had experienced the love and power of Jesus in her life, forgiving her sins, and this is what has sustained her for the whole of her life.

TURNING VULNERABILITY INTO AVAILABILITY

God then asks who is willing to go for him and Isaiah responds, 'Here am I. Send me!' (6:8). It is a beautifully simple statement of availability. But Isaiah says this not out of confidence but out of his vulnerability. He is aware of his weakness and fragility and that is what he is offering God. He is saying, 'Here I am, with all my sin, shame, weakness, fear and ignorance, but it is yours.' He is offering himself, not because of who he is and what he can offer, but because of who God is and what God has done for him.

The offer is made more powerful by the understanding of what he is offering. I have done quite a few weddings now, and it is always wonderful when the couple say those famous words to one another, 'For better, for worse, for richer, for poorer, in sickness and in health.' I know that, for some couples who are saying these words, so far things have mostly been better, richer and healthier. But for others it has been different. They have already gone through some tough times together, life-threatening illnesses, bereavements, real hardship, and when they say these words there is greater power and beauty in them because they really know what they are saying.

Isaiah is willing to go before he finds out any information about what exactly he is signing up to. It can be tempting to give God a few parameters, insisting that whatever we choose to do for him, God must at least provide an ample salary, the good opinion of those around us and maybe the opportunity for some exotic travel. But Isaiah simply says, 'Here am I. Send me!'

I once asked a helper at St Stephen's Society what made Jackie, the founder, stand out. He replied immediately, 'Her willingness. She is willing to do whatever God asks her.' She was willing to get on a boat that sailed around the world with no idea of her destination, praying that God would tell her when to get off. She was willing to get off the boat in Hong Kong even though she had no job, no money and nowhere to stay. She was willing to go into the Walled City, which the Chinese simply called 'Darkness', and work with the drug addicts, the sex workers and triad gang members, where the sewers overflowed and rats ran through the streets. She was willing to work with teenagers when there seemed to be no impact for years. And she has been willing to stay in Hong Kong and work there for over half a century, relying on God's faithful provision and miraculous power.

It is so easy to put limits on God, to insist on marriage, or a certain lifestyle, or certain places, but Isaiah is willing to offer himself completely and to do anything. God continues to ask this question, 'Who will go for us?' and each of us gets to respond to this question, 'Here am I. Send me!'

So Isaiah continues as a prophet, but now everything is different. His vision of God has been expanded. His awareness of his own weakness has grown. He has made himself totally available to the purposes of God.

What God calls him to is not easy. It is to go with a message that will not be heard (6:10) and he will have to keep speaking this message for decades until their land lies in ruins (6:11–13). His calling is not to be a success, but a failure. But Isaiah is not thinking about himself, for his mind has been filled with a vision of God himself. Isaiah's call does not emerge from self-discovery but from divine revelation, and particularly a vision of God as 'holy'. God's holiness means that his ways are not our ways. His perspective is not our perspective. His purposes and calling on our lives are not what we would have chosen for ourselves.

And yet his calling would have huge significance. He would not only prophesy destruction and loss, but also hope and renewal. He would speak not only of Israel, but of the coming Messiah. In placing himself into God's hands and his purposes, his ministry might have looked like a failure, but would play a part in a story which he would never have imagined.

Chapter 15

DISAPPOINTMENT

Jeremiah

Jeremiah 1

The word of the Lord came to me, saying,
'Before I formed you in the womb I knew you,
before you were born I set you apart;
I appointed you as a prophet to the nations.'

'Alas, Sovereign Lord,' I said, 'I do not know how to speak; I am
too young.'

But the Lord said to me, 'Do not say, "I am too young." You
must go to everyone I send you to and say whatever I command
you. Do not be afraid of them, for I am with you and will rescue
you,' declares the Lord.

Then the Lord reached out his hand and touched my mouth
and said to me, 'I have put my words in your mouth. See, today I
appoint you over nations and kingdoms to uproot and tear down,
to destroy and overthrow, to build and to plant.'

JEREMIAH 1:4-10

Get used to disappointment.

THE PRINCESS BRIDE*

One evening when we lived in Brighton, Tara had gone out and I
was at home doing some sewing. While I was sewing, I cut myself

---

* Rob Reiner, *The Princess Bride* (Twentieth Century Fox, 1987).

so badly it was clear that my life was in danger. It wasn't the pain that worried me; it was the loss of blood, which I was certain would be gushing from my finger. Our children were asleep upstairs; Tara was out, and I knew I didn't have very much time. I wondered about calling an ambulance, but they might not get to me in time. I managed to get to the first aid kit, desperately trying to find a bandage to stem the blood which I was convinced was coming out of my finger, wrapping it up, doing all I could to stay conscious.

I was stressed and in pain, but also secretly quite pleased. Tara is a wonderful person in so many ways, but one weakness I've discovered is that she's not very sympathetic when I'm ill, or when I've hurt myself. I've had some bad colds in my time, and I think Tara feels like these aren't as significant as say, giving birth, which she's done four times. But now I had something that was truly deserving of sympathy, and despite the trauma and slipping in and out of consciousness, I was secretly looking forward to the attention I would get from her when she got home.

When she arrived back, I told her what had happened, trying to stay strong for her sake, and wanting to make the most of what could be our final few moments together. Then I showed her the cut. Slowly, I unwrapped the bandage on my finger, being careful to keep the pressure on it, to stop the flow of blood. I unwound the whole bandage, discovering not a single drop of blood anywhere. It was a massive disappointment!

Life is full of disappointments. There are the everyday, little disappointments. The latest film, a party that you're not invited to, your sports team losing too often. And then there are the deep disappointments. There are failures, the things you've tried that haven't come off. There are relationships that ended badly or never happened at all. There are disappointments that take the form of loss: loss of work, loss of friends, tragedies, broken hearts and shattered dreams. Some disappointments are mild; others are devastating.

We can be disappointed with other people, those who have let us down, those who should have known better, with our friends, our parents or the Church. We can feel disappointed with our politicians and national leaders. We can feel disappointment with ourselves, that we are still struggling with the same issues without any apparent change, that we've messed up, that we are not who we could be or should be.

And then there's disappointment with God: for the prayers he hasn't answered, for the things we've been through when we feel he failed to protect us, for the times we have tried to do the right thing but it has all ended badly. We can feel the intense disappointment that life has not turned out as we had thought it would. As Fantine sings in Les Miserables, 'I had a dream my life would be so different from this hell I'm living, so different now from what it seemed ... Now life has killed the dream I dreamed.'*

Disappointment can be closely connected with calling, for there are times when our calling doesn't work out as we had hoped. Each time God has given me a clear sense of calling, to Oxford in my early twenties, to Brighton for thirteen years, and now in Brazil, I have seen so many wonderful things, beyond anything I could have hoped for or imagined. But there have also been some significant disappointments. In Oxford I had to drop out of university with chronic fatigue halfway through my studies, when I had felt like I was trying to follow Jesus and live obediently to him. In Brighton there was a property which we believed could be an ideal community house for people who were living on the streets and struggling with addiction. I used to pray for it, walking round it again and again, raising money and recruiting team for it, but it never quite happened. There have been many times when I've felt like I was trying to follow what God wanted for me, but things haven't turned out well, and I've been left confused, asking, 'What was that all about?' Sometimes the disappointment can make us question whether we were ever called in the first place.

* Claude-Michel Schönberg, *Les Miserables: a Musical* (H Leonard, 1988).

Disappointment can shake our identity and weaken our character, but more than anything it can cause us to lose our purpose. For disappointment is the non-fulfilment of our hopes or expectations. It literally means the loss of office, the loss of a purpose or role. But it can also bring about the renewal of our purpose and the reestablishment of our calling.

Jeremiah was a prophet chosen by God when the nation of Judah was about to go through the greatest disappointment they would ever experience. The Assyrian Empire, which had dominated the Ancient Near East for some time, was collapsing and the Babylon Empire was on the rise. This led to a series of political crises in Judah. The people of God were about to lose everything they loved, everything which had defined them as a nation: their king (the unbroken line of rulers descended from King David); the Temple (the place of worship and the presence of God); and their land (and therefore their independence). It was a time of national humiliation, and a political, economic, social and spiritual crisis. These key markers of their identity – their king, the temple and the land – had each been promised to them and then given to them by God. Now it would feel as though God had abandoned them and that his promises had failed. They had failed as a nation, their leaders had failed them and God had failed them.

As they begin to enter this time of disappointment, God calls Jeremiah as his prophet. This is a story of how our calling endures through disappointment.

PREPARED FOR DISAPPOINTMENT

First, God prepares us for disappointment. It can be tempting to try to avoid disappointment, hoping to protect ourselves from failure or rejection. We try to do only those things which we are good at. We avoid risks. We try to guarantee success. Or we resort to cynicism, or pessimism, thinking that by expecting the worst or learning not to care, we will be protected from disappointment. We might feel like it is God's role to protect us from disappointment, by guiding us along a life of constant success and acceptance. Therefore, when we look for our calling, it can be a way of looking for a purpose which is guaranteed to succeed.

But God calls Jeremiah not to avoid disappointment but to a purpose that will have to endure through disappointment. Parents generally try to protect their children from disappointment, whether consciously or unconsciously, but their role is actually to prepare their children to deal with the disappointments that life will inevitably bring. In the same way God's role is not to protect us from disappointment, but to prepare us for it.

He prepares us by saying, as he does to Jeremiah when he calls him, 'Do not be afraid ... I am with you and will rescue you' (Jeremiah 1:8). When God says, 'Do not be afraid' it is not a command not to feel afraid, but a command not to live out of fear, not to be ruled by fear, not to live fearful lives, not to try to avoid every disappointment. And God says, 'I am with you.' Often, we want to ask God, 'But will it be OK? Will it go well? Will it be a success?' But God only replies, 'I am with you.' The Babylonians would invade Judah. Jerusalem would fall. Jeremiah would be persecuted. In the tough times, the sad times and the disappointing times, which are sure to come, God promises to be with us. And he says, 'I ... will rescue you.' It is a reminder that there will be multiple dangers and situations from which we will need rescuing. And it is the reassurance that the disappointments, which we will inevitably face, will not have the last word.

HONEST IN DISAPPOINTMENT

Second, God helps us to be honest in the disappointment. If the first temptation is to try to avoid disappointment, the second is to try to pretend that we don't mind the disappointments, that we don't care, or even wanted this thing to happen, instead of allowing ourselves to feel the pain of what we are going through. Jeremiah is a book filled with heartbreaking honesty. He gives full vent to his personal pain and the anguish of a nation which is losing everything that it holds most dearly. But it is honesty without blame or bitterness. Blame is a common way that we discharge pain or discomfort. We cannot face the pain ourselves and so we project it on to other people, or on to God. But God invites us to be honest about our pain and frustration.

Nor must we become helpless. As God calls him, Jeremiah replies with two objections: that he is too young and that he doesn't know how to speak (1:6). He feels unable to do what God is calling him to do because of his youth and poor speaking skills. God responds by telling him that he's not too young. I can imagine Jeremiah waiting for the second part, where God would say to him, 'And you're an amazing speaker!' But God doesn't respond to this objection, which could imply that Jeremiah was right about his speaking abilities, but that they were irrelevant; that God is saying to him, 'It may be true that you're not great at speaking, but I will help you and turn your weakness into a strength.'

God rebukes him, telling him, 'Do not say, "I am too young"' (6:7). There is a difference between honesty, which is important and healthy, and complaining or grumbling, which are destructive. The Psalms are full of honesty; reading and praying them helps us articulate our pain to God. But when the Israelites go through the desert on the way to the Promised Land, they often complain and grumble, forgetting what God has already done for them and has promised to do for them in the future. We are supposed to be honest, but not helpless, to give God our pain and anguish, but never to forget his ability to work through us and in us. We grieve but do not give up. We can be hurt but mustn't discount ourselves from the purposes of God.

SECURE DESPITE DISAPPOINTMENT

Third, God secures us despite the disappointment. Intense disappointment can shake our identity. We can feel like we don't know who we are any more. But there is one who has known you from the start. As God calls Jeremiah, he reassures him: 'Before I formed you in the womb I knew you, before you were born I set you apart; I appointed you as a prophet to the nations' (1:5). Our calling is based on God's knowledge of us. God's purpose for our lives emerges not from self-knowledge but from being known by God. God knows us better than we know ourselves and the purpose of our lives is always partially obscured or unclear to us because we do not know ourselves as well as we could. But there is one who knows us completely and calls us to what is hidden from us.

And this knowledge is personal. God loves us through the disappointments of life. This means that we are not defined by our successes or failures. Our identity may be shaken by disappointment but not destroyed. For our identity is based on being loved by God. This is what secures us through the joys and pains of life. This is what sustains us through the ups and downs. We are loved before, during and after the successes and failures. Later Jeremiah writes, 'your words became to me a joy and the delight of my heart' (15:16, ESV), for it is God's voice, not our successes, which give us joy.

TRANSFORMED THROUGH DISAPPOINTMENTS

Fourth, God transforms us through the disappointment. Disappointment is a major way in which God transforms us, for it has the potential to strengthen us and give us empathy. God promises Jeremiah that he has been fortified, like an iron pillar or a bronze wall (1:18). He is going to be resilient, tough enough to be able to prophesy through these traumatic times. But he is not going to lose his sensitivity. He is going to continue to pour out his heart in emotional speeches. He is going to continue to feel keenly the pain of the nation. He is going to be strengthened in his resolve and character but softened in his heart.

The greatest leaders often manage to combine these two qualities of strength and empathy. They have 'soft hearts and hard feet'.* Abraham Lincoln was President of the United States through the American Civil War, the greatest moral, constitutional and political crisis that his country had ever faced. He saw the abolition of slavery legislation through and helped to bring healing to a divided nation. Yet he was a man who endured several disappointments. His mother died when he was nine and his beloved sister when he was nineteen. He suffered the disappointment of the death of a young woman he loved, then the refusal of a marriage proposal by another, both of which led to times of intense depression. He eventually married and had four sons, but three died: one aged four, one aged eleven, and one aged eighteen. And he failed to prevent his nation from descending into civil war. He wrote, 'I am now the most miserable man living. If what I feel were equally distributed to the whole human family, there would not be one cheerful face on the earth. Whether I shall ever be better I can not tell; I awfully forbode I shall not.'** And yet through these disappointments and his internal pain, Lincoln developed these two characteristics: empathy with the enslaved Americans, and the strength and resolve to abolish slavery and lead his country through civil war.

PURPOSE BEYOND DISAPPOINTMENT

Finally, God gives us a purpose which emerges through the other side of disappointment. Jeremiah is a book about intense disappointment, and yet it contains one of the most famous and hopeful verses about God's purpose for us: '"For I know the plans I have for you," declares the LORD, "plans to prosper you and not to harm you, plans to give you hope and a future"' (29:11). Even when everything seems to be

---

* From a sermon by Jackie Pullinger at Holy Trinity Brompton.
** Nassir Ghaemi, *A First-Rate Madness: Uncovering the Links between Leadership and Mental Illness* (Penguin, 2011), p71.

lost, God continues to have plans for his people. There are good and hopeful plans which God knows and will fulfil.

Jeremiah is a book of huge *dis*appointment, and yet it starts with God saying to Jeremiah, 'I appointed you' (1:5). No matter what is going to take place, this appointment will remain. God's calling on us is stronger than our disappointment. His appointment trumps our disappointment.

Later God will bring a new purpose out of Israel's disappointment. Disappointment brings one thing to an end so that something better and more beautiful can grow up in its place. In this period of Israel's history they will lose all those things which were most precious to them as a nation. They would lose their king, the descendants of David, and would never again have their own king. They would lose their temple, the place of the presence of God, and though rebuilt much later, never again would the glory of God fill it. And they would lose their land, which had been promised to them, where they had lived in freedom and security, and though some would return from exile in the future, from now on they would almost always be ruled by other empires.

But out of this acute national disappointment would come something far greater. From the loss of a human king would come hope of a divine king – the Messiah – God himself ruling his people. Out of the loss of the temple would come hope for God's Spirit poured out on all people. And from the loss of the land there emerged a new hope of the kingdom of God, stretching out across the whole world and including every nation and language and people. God can turn disappointment into a new appointment. Sometimes he disappoints us so that we might be reappointed.

Lincoln's great purpose to bring about the abolition of a great injustice, the reunification and healing of a nation, remained despite the disappointments. By the end of the Civil War he had lost none of his hope. In his second inaugural address, he said, 'With malice toward none, with charity for all, with firmness in the right as God gives us to see the right, let us strive on to finish the work we are in, to bind up the nation's wounds, to care for him who shall have borne the battle and for his widow and his orphan, to do all which may achieve and cherish a just and lasting peace among ourselves and with all nations.'*

Jesus did not avoid disappointment, but went to the cross, which looked like the total failure of his life and ministry, the total failure of politics and politicians, the failure of religion and religious leaders. He expressed his apparent disappointment, crying out from the cross, 'My God, my God why have you forsaken me?'** It looked like a permanent disappointment. And yet through the resurrection, as Paul writes, Jesus was 'appointed the Son of God.'*** Through his resurrection Jesus overcame disappointment forever. The resurrection reassures us that disappointment can never define us, deflate us or defeat us, for he is the appointed one, and in him we too are appointed for a great purpose.

* Ghaemi, p76.
**Matthew 27:46.
*** Romans 1:4.

Chapter 16

RELUCTANCE

Jonah
Jonah 1 – 4

The word of the LORD came to Jonah son of Amittai: 'Go to the great city of Nineveh and preach against it, because its wickedness has come up before me.'

But Jonah ran away from the LORD and headed for Tarshish.

JONAH 1:1-3

Everybody runs.

MINORITY REPORT*

When God calls us, it changes everything, giving purpose to our lives, meaning to our work and significance to our relationships. It makes our lives a great adventure. But calling also exposes our weaknesses, our reluctance and our low expectations. Jonah is one of the most successful but least impressive figures in the Bible. Through him some non-Jewish sailors are converted to faith in the God of Israel, the capital city of a hostile empire is transformed and a humanitarian disaster is avoided, but it all happens through a flawed and reluctant prophet. This is hugely encouraging, for it means that God's purpose for your life is greater than your weakness, stronger than your reluctance and it is beyond your expectations.

---

* Steven Spielberg, *Minority Report* (DreamWorks Pictures, 2002).

GREATER THAN OUR WEAKNESS

Jonah is not an impressive character. He is stubborn, disobedient and selfish. When God calls him to go and preach to the people of Nineveh at the heart of the Assyrian Empire, he runs away (Jonah 1:3). This is perhaps understandable for the Assyrians were a particularly violent people and would eventually invade the nation of Israel. However, when the boat he is fleeing on goes through a storm and begins to sink, everyone else on board works frantically to save their lives (and Jonah's), but Jonah is asleep below deck (1:5). While the sailors are praying to be rescued and ask him to pray, Jonah remains silent (1:6). Then later, when Jonah eventually preaches to the Ninevites, warning them of their impending destruction, they repent en masse and God forgives them, but Jonah is furious. Perhaps he thinks Nineveh doesn't deserve God's mercy or perhaps he thinks God's mercy makes it seem as though his prophecy that Nineveh would be destroyed had been wrong all along (4:1). Deep inside, he would rather that all the Ninevites die, than that all the Ninevites repent and be saved.

Despite all these things, God works powerfully through him, because God's purpose for our lives is not limited by our weaknesses. It is not limited by our physical weaknesses, or our moral weaknesses or by the limitations of our personalities.

Jonah does not appear to be the obvious choice for a mission to Nineveh. His name means 'dove', a species of bird which is easily startled and has strong homing instincts. In addition, we learn from 2 Kings (the only information we have of Jonah outside the book which bears his name) that he had a role in restoring the borders of Israel,* which might suggest a desire to keep foreigners out. He likes home and dislikes foreigners. So God calls him to move away from home and spend time in a foreign capital city.

God calls Jonah to do something which doesn't seem to be a

---

* 2 Kings 14:25.

good fit for his personality: to go beyond home, to reach out beyond the boundaries of Israel. He wants to be at the centre but is called to the edge. Jonah didn't seem to have had a 'heart' for Nineveh. He didn't really do 'foreign.' And yet that is exactly where God calls him.

In the Bible it is nearly always surprising whom God uses for his purposes. The old and childless Abraham is called to be a father of many nations, the fearful Gideon to be a military leader, the virgin Mary to have a child. Paul, the most Jewish of Jews, was called to be an apostle to the Gentiles and lead the advance of Christianity beyond the borders of Judaism.

The same is true in the history of the church. DL Moody, the uneducated American evangelist in the nineteenth century, who left school at 14 and who was always aware of his lack of learning, was the one whom God called to Cambridge University in 1886 and who had such an impact on that group of students that it led to the Cambridge Seven taking the gospel to China and beyond. David Wilkerson was a country pastor, with no experience of urban ministry, but God called him to go to reach the gangs of New York in the 1950s. Jackie Pullinger was a student at the Royal College of Music, and God called her to reach the triad gangs and heroin addicts of the Walled City in Hong Kong.

Of course, God also uses our natural gifts, skills and abilities. Jonah is a prophet, so it makes sense to choose a prophet to go and speak to the Ninevites. But God uses both Jonah's strengths and his weaknesses.

God's call on our lives is greater than our weakness, but this does not mean that our weaknesses do not matter. They matter hugely. The weaknesses and mistakes of those who have been called by God always have consequences, often serious ones. Jonah's rebellion will mean that lots of people lose their possessions as they try to stop the boat from sinking (1:5). Jonah's pride will mean that he gets sunstroke (4:8). Our weaknesses do matter. We can hurt people and miss important opportunities. But they do not limit the purposes of

God. Our flaws are not enough to thwart his purposes.

The weaknesses and flaws you see in yourself are not a limit on what God is able to do through you, nor are the weaknesses you see in others a limit on what God will accomplish through them. For we have a Heavenly Father who works his purposes through you, though you discount yourself, and through those around you, though you might discount them.

STRONGER THAN OUR RELUCTANCE

Jonah says 'No' to God. He runs away physically, and he runs away emotionally. When God calls him to go to Nineveh (just across the Tigris from present-day Mosul in Iraq), he decides to get on a ship to Tarshish (possibly on the south coast of Spain), as if to try to get as far away from where he is called to as possible. He also goes to sleep on the boat. It's as if he's trying to shut himself off from God's voice and everything that is happening around him.

In some ways we are always running away, if not physically then certainly emotionally. We can use constant work, distractions, screens, the people around us, anything we can find to silence the voice which might be calling us to do something we don't want to do. We are often reluctant to follow the call of God. There may be times when God calls us and it is accompanied by peace or excitement or enthusiasm, but normally it seems to be accompanied with fear and resistance. Moses, Gideon, Isaiah and Esther were all resistant to God's call. Rarely in the Bible do we find someone whom God calls who then responds with delight and gratitude. There is almost always some kind of resistance.

The former Archbishop of Canterbury and theologian Rowan Williams writes that if you're trying to reconnect with the purpose for your life then the crucial question is not what would be an ideal fit for your passions, gifts, experience and personality, but what are you running from? 'What am I denying, what am I refusing to see in myself? What am I trying to avoid?"

And yet God is able to overcome our reluctance. Often, he does this through storms. God sends storms to shake us from our complacency and force us to question the direction of our lives. Here God sends a great 'wind' (1:4). The Hebrew for wind here is '*ruach*', which can mean wind, or spirit, or the Spirit. It hints that the Spirit of God was in the storm which was sent to restore the purpose which God had for Jonah. God uses the storms of life to get us back on track, to realign us to his purposes and remember the one who calls us.

At other times it is a word from God which overcomes our reluctance. When God first calls Jonah, he says, 'Arise, go to Nineveh, that great city' (1:2, NJKV). When the captain goes to find the sleeping Jonah in the bottom of the boat, he uses the same word, '*Arise*, call on your God' (1:6, NJKV). The captain unknowingly used the same word which God had used when he called Jonah, reminding him of his original calling. It was an echo from the past, forcing Jonah to recall something which had been ignored or lost. We can easily forget the words which God has said to us in the past, but then suddenly something happens, we read a verse in the Bible, we hear a sermon, someone prays for us and uses a phrase we had forgotten, and it all brings us back to the original word from God.

Ultimately, God overcomes Jonah's reluctance by loving him and saving him. Jonah's eventual yes to God emerges because God rescues him. After being thrown overboard by the other passengers, and being swallowed by a large fish, he cries out from the belly of the fish in gratitude for the God who loves him and saves him (2:1–9). In the end, it is not the fear of another storm but an awareness of God's grace which motivates Jonah. Later Paul will write, 'in view of God's mercy ... offer your bodies as a living sacrifice."* It is our experience of the grace of God which ultimately motivates us to offer ourselves for God's purposes.

* Rowan Williams, *Open to Judgement* (Darton, Longman and Todd, 1994), p175.
** Romans 12:1.

God's love is stronger than our reluctance. For love is the only power that can overcome our reluctance without reducing our freedom. In fact, it increases our freedom, giving us the freedom to say yes. God's love can melt our hearts and bring us back to where we should be and what we should be doing.

BEYOND OUR EXPECTATIONS

Jonah's trip to Nineveh does not turn out as he hopes or expects. Having eventually agreed to go to this great city, it appears that Jonah expected that, having warned them of total destruction, the city would be totally destroyed and Jonah would be vindicated as a true prophet. However, God forgives and restores the Ninevites and it perhaps looked like Jonah had got it wrong.

In the stories of calling in the Bible, God rarely gives much information about what will happen to those he calls. When he calls Moses to rescue the people of Israel from Egypt and take them into the Promised Land, he fails to mention some important details: Pharoah's opposition, the ten plagues which will be necessary to force Pharaoh's hand, the moment they are nearly wiped out by the Egyptian army and need a miracle to cross the Red Sea, the forty years in the desert, the battles against enemies and the constant complaints of the Israelites. God simply tells him to go to Egypt and take the Israelites to the Promised Land. It is similar when God called Abram in Ur, or gave dreams to the teenage Joseph, or called Mary to be the mother of the Messiah. God doesn't tell us much, probably because we wouldn't agree to it if he did. God's purpose for our lives is almost always much harder and much better than we expect. This is certainly true of marriage, of parenting and of planting churches.

For Jonah it is harder because it means confronting his own pride, prejudices and weaknesses. God's call on our life often takes us to places where our weaknesses are exposed, and where we experience all kinds of unexpected challenges. But it is also greater than we expect. For Jonah it will mean the transformation of an entire city.

When God calls us, it is to the unknown, the unpredictable and the unexpected. So when we are called to something new, it is tempting to ask God, 'OK, I'll do this, but is it going to be OK?' to which sometimes God replies, 'I make no such promise.' We ask, 'But do you promise that it will go well?' and he may reply, 'I make no such promise.' We ask, 'But will I look good at the end of it? Will people know that I've done this? Will I get to see the results of my work?' and the reply might come again, 'I make no such promise.'

But the consequences of our obedience, even though it is so often reluctant, will be far greater than we could have ever imagined. We respond to God's voice unaware of what God is going to do through us. Abraham did not realize that he was starting God's work of redemption which would culminate in God himself coming to his own people. Ruth perhaps thought that she was simply looking after an older relative and then taking a risk in trying to find a husband; she had no idea that she was starting a dynasty of kings for Israel which would pave the way for the Messiah. The Old Testament prophets often thought that they were speaking into their current situations, challenging the people and calling them back to their God, but they were also speaking of a greater reality of the Son of God who would come to save the world.

Jonah thought that he was wrestling with a mission from God to a city he didn't like, unaware that he was part of a much greater story. Hundreds of years later, another prophet would arise, and when Jesus was asked by the Pharisees for a sign, he would give them only this: the sign of Jonah.* That flawed and reluctant prophet got to be a sign of the greatest act of redemption for the world. The one who wished a city wouldn't be saved for the sake of his reputation would become a sign of one who gave up not only his reputation, but his

* Matthew 12:39.

life, so that the whole world might be saved.

This story is about God working for his purposes, despite our character flaws, our reluctance and our false expectations. But more than this it is about a God who never stops loving us and is always wanting to draw us closer. The book of Jonah doesn't finish with the conversion of Nineveh, but with God's continued efforts to help Jonah in his relationship with him. For God is not interested only in Jonah's actions, he is working on Jonah's character and his relationship with Jonah. He doesn't just want Jonah the prophet; he wants Jonah the person. The purpose of your life is not just to do various tasks, but it is also to become the person that God made you to be and to love the God who loves you perfectly.

Jonah gets so much wrong in this story, but he gets one thing right. He eventually says 'yes' to God even though he said 'no' before. When I proposed to Tara in January 2009, she didn't say 'yes' at first. But later, crucially, she said 'yes' and it changed everything. A 'yes' to God, even if you've been running for years, changes everything. So, say yes to the purpose that God has for your life, and embrace a purpose which is greater than your weaknesses, stronger than your reluctance and beyond your expectations.

PART FOUR

Embrace

Chapter 17

OVERCOMING FEAR AND SAYING YES

Mary
Luke 1:26–38

'I am the Lord's servant,' Mary answered. 'May your word to me be fulfilled.'

LUKE 1:38

In these few simple words, the greatest and most decisive act of faith in history took place.

RANIERO CANTALAMESSA*

Now we come to my favourite story of calling in the Bible: Mary's beautiful response to God's call. It's so beautiful because it is so simple. The angel Gabriel visits a young girl in Nazareth, telling her that she will bear the Messiah. And Mary says 'yes' to God. This is the gateway into a life of purpose – saying yes to Jesus. For God's call is like an invitation, or maybe more like a marriage proposal, and our role is simply to say 'yes'.

But saying yes is not so easy. For to say yes to God we need to overcome our fear. Accepting God's call on our lives always means having to overcome something. For Moses it was his past mistakes.

---

* Father Raniero Cantalamessa, 'First Advent Sermon 2019: Blessed is she who Believed! Mary in the Annunciation', Vatican City, 6 December 2019, cantalamessa.org (accessed May 2024).

For Ruth it was being a foreigner. For Samuel it was his youth. For David it was criticism. For Jonah it was his reluctance. There's always something we need to overcome. And very often that obstacle will be fear. Saying 'yes' to the purposes of God for our lives means having to face our fears. That's why, in so many stories of calling, God says to the one he is calling, 'Do not be afraid.' He says it to Abraham, Isaac, Jacob, Joshua, Gideon, Jeremiah, Ezekiel, Joseph, Mary, Paul and John.*

Why is fear connected to our calling? First, because God's call is disruptive. It can disrupt our location, as it does when God commands Abraham to go to a new land. It can disrupt our work, as it does when Jesus calls the first disciples to leave their fishing nets or tax-collecting booths and come and follow him. It often disrupts our comfort and our stability, our routine and our lifestyle. It can disrupt our finances, as it does when Jesus calls the disciples to leave the sources of their income.

And it can disrupt our relationships. For Mary this call was a severe disruption to her relationships. Mary was engaged to be married to Joseph, whom we know was kind, honourable, discreet, practical and descended from King David (he sounds like the ideal husband!). But now Mary was going to have to tell him that she was pregnant and assume that this relationship would be all over. And she would likely be shunned by her family.

It would disrupt her reputation. The good girl, from a good family, would now be a teenager, pregnant before she was married, at a time when that was intensely shameful. There would be slurs circulating around her for the rest of her life.

It would disrupt her safety. There was a chance she would be stoned to death for adultery. It would disrupt her plans. This was not how things were supposed to go. This was not what she wanted. This was not what she expected. And yet she says 'yes.'

* Genesis 15:1; 26:24; 46:3; Joshua 1:9; Judges 6:23; Jeremiah 1:8; Ezekiel 2:6; Matthew 1:20; Luke 1:30; Acts 18:9; Revelation 1:17.

The second reason it is frightening is that we don't normally feel qualified to do what God calls us to do. Mary says, 'How will this be ... since I am a virgin?' (Luke 1:34). She hasn't got the qualifications for this role. As we've seen before, God's call is almost always to go beyond our strengths and experience, beyond what we feel we can do. For me, God's call has exposed all kinds of issues like disorganization, slow decision-making, lack of energy, the need to please people, indiscretion and the tendency to keep people at a distance.

The call of God is always frightening. It means the loss of control, the risk of failure, the loss of comfort and the letting go of what is known. And this fear can stop us saying yes to God. Fear often closes us off, causing us to withdraw from God and push him away and to put walls up to try to keep ourselves safe. It can stop us embracing God's call on our lives.

So God says to us, 'Do not be afraid.' Again, this is not a command not to have fearful feelings, for we cannot control our feelings. It means, 'Don't be ruled by your fear. Don't let fear dictate your actions.' It is not a command to eradicate our feelings, but to say 'yes' to God even when we are afraid. Being called by God means facing our fears. We are afraid and we say yes anyway.

And the more significant the calling, the greater the fear. Mary is not slightly fearful here. The word used of her fear is *diaterrasso* (1:29) which is often translated 'greatly troubled'. In the previous verses, we read about how when an angel appeared to the priest Zechariah, he is described as *terrasso*, which means 'frightened'. Mary's fear is *dia-terrasso*, where *dia* means thoroughly. This word *diaterrasso* is only used once in the whole of the New Testament. Zechariah is afraid, but Mary is terrified. There is no one in all the New Testament who is described as being more terrified than Mary is at this moment. And yet she still says yes.

She's also confused. She 'wonders' (1:29). The word used is *dialogistai* which means she doesn't understand what's going on. She asks, 'How is this going to happen?' (1:34). It doesn't make sense and she cannot work out what is going on. And yet she still says yes.

And it is not just any 'yes'. The word she uses when she says, 'May your word to me be fulfilled' (1:38), is *genoito*. It's in the optative mood, which means that it expresses desire.* It signifies that she doesn't say 'yes' reluctantly. It is not an 'OK', or 'I suppose so', or 'If I must'. It's more like, 'Let's do this', 'Bring it on', 'Make it so'. It is not a partial yes; it is a full yes. She is not just accepting God's call; she is embracing it.

The one who in all the Scriptures is most afraid is also the one who most fully embraces the call of God. She is the person most filled with fear, and yet she gives the fullest 'yes'. How does this happen?

Mary is able to say yes through being full of grace and full of faith, and from the example of what God has done in the lives of others. She had been filled with something deeper than the fear, was attached to something stronger than the fear and was inspired by the example of someone around her to overcome the fear.

FILLED WITH SOMETHING DEEPER: GRACE

Mary was able to say yes because of the grace that was stronger than the fear. The angel announces to Mary that she is 'highly favoured' (1:28). The word used is *kecharitomene*. It is in the perfect tense, which means that something has happened in the past which has created a reality in the present. It could be translated 'you have been filled with grace'. It suggests that God has done something in the past which has prepared her for this moment. And the angel says, 'The Lord is with you' (1:28). It is the presence of God with Mary that makes her response possible.

* Father Raniero Cantalamessa, *Mary, Mirror of the Church* (Liturgical Press, 1992), p42.

This is essential for taking hold of God's call. It is the promise that God has been working within you to prepare you for this very moment, so there is more in you than you realize. You are prepared for what he calls you to do, for God gives us everything we need when we need it. He pays for what he orders. Don't be afraid, because God has been preparing you for what he has called you to do, and he is with you.

John writes, 'There is no fear in love, but perfect love drives out fear.'* It seems God had placed a love within Mary which was stronger than the fear. She was able to say yes because, though the fear went deep, the grace went deeper. She was filled with something stronger and deeper than the fear. So do not try to not feel afraid; instead let the grace of God go deeper than the fear.

On that day in January 2009, when I was trying to persuade Tara to marry me, the main obstacle for Tara was fear. She said that she felt a range of emotions about marriage, but the dominant feeling was fear – the fear of getting it wrong, the fear of making a mistake. She said that it was as if ninety percent of her emotions about marrying me were characterized by fear. However, right at the bottom, much smaller than the fear, but much more solid and trustworthy, was something else, the knowledge that this was the right thing for her and for us. In the end, she managed to trust that solid reality which existed in the midst of all the fear. There was something deeper and something stronger than the fear.

This is how we can overcome fear and embrace God's call on our lives, not by trying to stop ourselves feeling afraid, but by connecting to the grace of God which has been given to us, which goes so much deeper and which is much more trustworthy than the fear.

---

* 1 John 4:18, ESV.

INSPIRED BY THOSE AROUND HER:
COMMUNITY

Mary was able to say yes, because she was inspired by what God had done in another person's life. The angel says to her, 'Even Elizabeth your relative is going to have a child in her old age, and she who was said to be unable to conceive is in her sixth month.' (1:36) The angel points Mary to an example of God's work. It was a demonstration both of God's kindness, for Elizabeth had longed for a child, and God's power, for Elizabeth was unable to have children. It would also have reminded Mary of some of the great stories in Israel's history, where God intervened to give children to those who were struggling to conceive, and where their situation seemed hopeless, like the births of Isaac, Samson and Samuel. In each case God had performed a miracle and achieved great things through those children.

We, too, can be inspired to embrace our calling by looking at the stories of the past, the stories we read in the Bible, the great examples from church history and those around us in our own lives who have experienced God's power and grace. We do not make these decisions in a vacuum, but as part of a wider story in which we see God acting kindly and powerfully again and again.

Mary will later prepare for this crucial moment in her life by going to spend time with Elizabeth. She goes to a place where a miracle has already taken place. Time spent in places full of stories of God's miracles help us to embrace God's call, particularly when we feel like it would take a miracle to be able to do what God asks us to do. I'm not sure we would have found it so easy to accept the call to Brazil if we hadn't gone to Hong Kong two years before, spending time in a context in which there were so many stories of radically transformed lives, and so many examples of people who had given up everything to follow Jesus.

Mary was inspired by the example of Elizabeth. Since then, billions have been inspired by the example of Mary. So we make these decisions, inspired by those who have gone before us and by those who have embraced God's call around us. And, hopefully, we then become an example to others.

ATTACHED TO SOMETHING STRONGER: FAITH

Mary was also able to say 'yes' because she had attached herself to something stronger than the fear. She describes herself as a 'servant of the Lord' (1:38). In other words, she was placing herself in the hands of the Lord, entrusting herself to him. The antidote to fear is not the removal of what is frightening, but to attach ourselves to something, or someone, stronger than the fear.

Our purpose is not within us but outside of us. Paul writes, 'we know that in all things God works for the good of those who love him, who have been called according to *his* purpose.'* Mary does not so much discover her own purpose here, as she discovers the purpose of her son. And she attaches herself to this purpose. This is the faith that overcomes fear.

Hudson Taylor founded the China Inland Mission, becoming one of the most significant missionaries of the nineteenth century and having a profound impact on the spread of Christianity in China. However, in June 1865 Hudson Taylor was burnt out. He was thirty-three years old, and back in England due to ill health after working for another mission in China for six years. He had begun to hear the whisper of God saying to him, 'I intend to evangelize inland China. If you will walk with me, I will do it through you.' But he was consumed with fear. He was afraid of failure. He was afraid that he would burn out the other missionaries and that they would blame him, that they might die of starvation and leave wives without husbands and children fatherless.

And so even though he heard God's voice say 'go', he found

---

* Romans 8:28.

himself saying, 'no'. He felt heavy and burdened. On 25 June he went down from London to Brighton to stay with a friend. He went to church but hated the service, so he left early and went wandering out on the beach, which was deserted at that time because most people went to church on Sunday mornings.

As he walked along the beach, he had a sudden revelation: 'Why, if we are obeying the Lord, the responsibility rests with *Him*, not with us'. He prayed to God, '*Thou*, Lord. *Thou* shalt have the burden. All the responsibility lies with Thee, Lord Jesus. I surrender. *Thou* shalt direct, care for, guide me, and those who labour with me. I *will* ask for the workers to come forward.'

He wrote in his Bible the next day, 'Prayed for twenty-four willing skilful labourers at Brighton, June 25, 1865. All was joy and peace. I felt as if I could fly up the hill … And how I did sleep that night! My dear wife thought Brighton had done wonders for me, and it had.'*

SAYING YES

Saying yes to God in this way makes all kinds of things possible. This word *genoito*, which Mary uses, reminds us of the creation of the world, when God says, 'Let there be light'.** This is not just a full yes but a *creative* yes. It was a yes that had the power to bring God himself into his own creation, into human history. Every time we say yes to God, new things are brought into being – new dreams, new visions, new possibilities, new realities.

It was also an *eternal* yes. Mary never stopped saying yes to God. She was the first person in the world to say yes to Jesus. She was still there at the cross. She witnessed the resurrection. She is with her son now, still saying yes to the Son of God.

* John Pollock, *Hudson Taylor and Maria: A Match Made in Heaven* (Christian Focus Publications, 1996), p126.
** Genesis 1:3.

JOY AND PAIN

The angel greets Mary with the word, 'Greetings' (1:28). It is literally *Chaire* or 'Rejoice.' This call is above any other calling in the Bible: to carry the Son of God and be his mother. It held huge risks and meant so much sacrifice and pain for Mary. It can be painful to say yes to God. When Jesus said yes to his Father, in the Garden of Gethsemane shortly before his death, he was in agony. After Jesus' birth the old and devout Simeon would take Jesus in his arms and, addressing Mary, predict that 'a sword will pierce your own soul too' (2:35). This is not an easy calling.

But this calling is also a gift which brings joy, and she will respond by singing out to God, 'my Spirit rejoices in God my Saviour' (1:47). It is a reminder that God loves you and wants you to be happy. God doesn't call us because he hates us and wants to make our lives worse. He doesn't call us because he needs us and wouldn't know what to do if we were not there to help him. He calls us because he loves us and wants to include us in his wonderful purposes for the world.

In a wedding service a husband and wife give themselves to one another completely, making promises which will entail making huge sacrifices and leaving behind all they've known before, yet it is not a moment of sadness but of huge joy. It is the same when we say yes to God. Hudson Taylor experienced that joy when he finally said yes to God. Jackie Pullinger used to get the feeling of it being her birthday whenever she went into the Walled City.

Though it is often painful and difficult, full of challenges and battles, there is no greater joy than saying yes to the call of God.

Chapter 18

FACING FAILURE AND REDISCOVERING PURPOSE

Peter
John 21

When they had finished eating, Jesus said to Simon Peter, 'Simon son of John, do you love me more than these?'

'Yes, Lord,' he said, 'you know that I love you.'

Jesus said, 'Feed my lambs.'

Again Jesus said, 'Simon son of John, do you love me?'

He answered, 'Yes, Lord, you know that I love you.'

Jesus said, 'Take care of my sheep.'

The third time he said to him, 'Simon son of John, do you love me?'

Peter was hurt because Jesus asked him the third time, 'Do you love me?' He said, 'Lord, you know all things; you know that I love you.'

Jesus said, 'Feed my sheep.'

JOHN 21:15–17

There is a way to be good again.

THE KITE RUNNER*

---

* Khaled Hosseini, *The Kite Runner* (Riverhead Books, 2003), p2.

Sometimes we need to discover our purpose. We are looking for meaning and purpose, wondering what God might want us to do with our lives. But there are other times when we need to *rediscover* our purpose. We once had a purpose. We felt called. But then something went wrong, and we have lost our way, got distracted by the busyness and stresses of life, and we have lost sight of what we were aiming to do with our lives. Or we've messed up, making terrible mistakes and everything feels like it has fallen apart. When we've forgotten who we are and what we were supposed to be doing, when we've lost what we once had, Jesus is still able to renew and restore our purpose.

This is what we find in this story of Simon Peter. For Peter had lost his way. Three years earlier he had been a fisherman called Simon, when Jesus had miraculously enabled him to catch a huge number of fish, calling him to be his disciple and to become a 'fisher of people.' He had left everything to follow Jesus. Later, he had been given a new name, Peter, or 'rock'. He had been one of Jesus' closest friends, one of only three who got to see the Transfiguration and the raising of Jairus's daughter from the dead. He had helped Jesus multiply food, heal the sick and cast out demons. He had been taught to pray. He had claimed that he would follow Jesus even if everyone else fell away, even if it meant dying with him.*

But then everything had fallen apart. After Jesus was arrested, Peter had followed him to the high priest's courtyard and had ended up denying that he knew Jesus three times.** He had lost his nerve at a moment of crisis, doing the very thing he had promised to Jesus and to himself that he would never do, denying that he knew Jesus, protecting his own life, instead of laying it down for the one he loved.

He was supposed to stand firm like a rock but had crumbled under pressure. He was called to be a fisher of men and women, but now he had gone back to being a fisher of fish. For when things had fallen apart, he returned to what he knew and was good at, catching fish, but

---

* Luke 5:1–11; Matthew 16:18; 17:1; Mark 5:37; 14:29, 31.
** John 18:17, 25, 27.

even this was going wrong, and he had caught nothing (21:3).

But Jesus was about to restore his purpose, renewing and transforming his calling. For Peter is going to move from being a fisher of men to being a shepherd of people.

GOING BACK TO THE START

Sometimes we need to go back to where it all began. This is what Jesus does with Peter. He had first called him while he was fishing unsuccessfully, intervening to enable him to catch a huge quantity of fish. Now Jesus repeats the miracle, reminding Peter of how it all began. And then over breakfast he calls him 'Simon', his old name. He is taking him back to the start.

It is easy to get disorientated, distracted, discouraged or disillusioned, and to lose track of what God has called us to do. It is easy to mess up and feel like there is no way back. When this happens, it is helpful to go back to the start, to try to remember 'why did I become a teacher in the first place' – or a nurse, or a politician, or a musician? Before I became hardened, or discouraged, before I started making these mistakes, why did I decide to do this in the first place? It can be helpful in a marriage too, to go back to those first moments when you fell in love or felt God calling you to be together. Frequently, in both Brighton and in Rio, I would try to go back to our original vision, to what we felt God had called us to do.

When something goes wrong with a phone or computer, the answer is almost always the same: restart it. Turn it off, and then turn it back on again. It's the same with our lives when we've drifted off track. We need to restart. This is what Jesus does for Peter here. He resets him.

FACING THE PAST

For Jesus to restore Peter's calling, he needs to help him to face his past, to deal with the regrets and shame from the previous weeks.

Just as Moses had to return to Egypt, the geographical location of his painful past, so Peter has to return, emotionally and spiritually, to his own failure and shame.

In the hours before and after Jesus' arrest, Peter had just made a series of increasingly bad decisions. After a stressful and exhausting week, in the middle of the night, under intense pressure, Peter had cracked. First, he had fallen asleep when Jesus had asked him to keep watch with him and pray. Then he had attacked one of those arresting Jesus, cutting off his ear. Peter, who had been there during the Sermon on the Mount, when Jesus had taught them about loving their enemies, turning the other cheek and not resisting those who attack them, had thought the best way to apply Jesus' teaching was to grab a sword and attack people. Finally, he had followed Jesus to the high priest's courtyard, finding himself again surrounded by hostile people, and three times had denied that he knew Jesus. And then the cockerel crowed. It had all happened exactly as Jesus had predicted when Peter had insisted that he would never fail him.

There seem to be two main ways that we can react to pressure and stress. Sometimes we lash out, expressing anger, bitterness and hostility to those around us. Out of our own pain we hurt other people. Alternatively, we compromise, trying to hide away, going along with the crowd, trying to keep our heads down and ensure that people still like us and we survive. I tend to go for this second option, agreeing with whoever I'm talking to, not wanting to cause problems, to ensure that people don't stop liking me. So we either fight or we hide away. Peter manages to do both these things in quick succession, first attacking the high priest's servant, and then hiding away in the courtyard of the high priest. These are both reactions to the pressure and pain of his situation. And both reactions are the denial of Jesus.

So, like all of us, he had a past. He had failed. And the memory of his failure would have been unavoidable, for cockerels were everywhere in the Holy Land. Every morning, as they crowed, he would have been reminded of what he had done. And his denials had taken place around a fire. Again, fires would have been part of daily life for them all. All these constant reminders of his mistakes. Unmistakable sounds, unavoidable smells, reminding him of his failure.

For Jesus to reestablish Peter's calling, Jesus had first to deal with his past. So Jesus confronts him gently but firmly. He lights a fire to remind him of that night. It was early in the morning, so there were probably cockerels crowing in the background. And he asks him three questions, just as he had been asked that night that he had failed.

'Triggering' refers to the strong emotional reaction when someone is made to remember something bad that has happened in the past. Often we try to avoid these triggers. But here Jesus deliberately 'triggers' Peter. Jesus deliberately puts his finger on the most painful part within Peter, so that he can heal and restore it. Sometimes Jesus deliberately creates conditions to bring painful experiences to the surface – memories we would rather stay hidden – so that he can deal with them once and for all.

Jesus 'triggers' Peter, but he does not shame him. We don't know whether at this point Peter has told the other disciples what he had done. I think he may well not have told them. And so Jesus brings up what happened in a way that Peter would understand, but the others wouldn't. So, he lights a fire, and he does it as the cockerels were crowing, and he asks three questions. But he doesn't say to Peter, 'Come on! Why don't you tell everyone what you did? Remember, you told everyone here that even if they fell away, you wouldn't. Is that what happened?' No, Jesus confronts him, but he does not shame him.

Jesus then heals Peter's past by reminding him of his love for him. He gives him food, as a sign of friendship. The questions Jesus asks Peter give him the opportunity to reaffirm his love for Jesus. And out of this restoration of relationship, he gives him a new purpose.

Your past is not an obstacle to what God can work through you.

The cross not only removes our sin; it also restores our purpose. If we allow Jesus into our pasts to redeem and restore them, he will bring meaning from our mistakes and purpose out of our pasts.

We know that Jesus' approach with Peter worked, because we have the gospel accounts of Peter's denial of Jesus. There seem to be three main ways that we can respond to our mistakes. The first is avoidance. We try to avoid the person we've hurt, or the place where it happened. Peter does not avoid the past. When he sees Jesus, he dives into the water and swims towards him, not away from him. He moves towards the one he has hurt.

The second approach is denial, pretending to yourself that it didn't happen, and making sure no one finds out. Peter could well have thought to himself, 'As the leader of this movement, it's important the others trust me, and if they knew what had happened then the whole thing might fall apart, so it's best for everyone if no one knows. After all, I'm forgiven.' But this is not Peter's approach. It was not inevitable that the other disciples would find out what had happened. We know what happened because Peter told people. And it's in all four gospels. Peter made sure that whenever the story of Jesus' death was told, his failure was also told.

The third response is to try to justify ourselves, by presenting the best possible interpretation of what has happened, putting ourselves in the best light we can. Peter could have done this. There were all kinds of ways for him to justify his actions. He might have stressed the necessity of his actions, for when Jesus had been arrested, everyone's life had been in danger. If they had all been caught, that would have been the end of their movement. It was important for at least someone to survive to continue Jesus' work. He could have emphasized his courage, for though the others had run away, he had bravely gone 'under cover', cleverly disguising himself as someone else, to stay close to Jesus. And he could have denied that he did anything wrong. My brother, who trained as a lawyer, suggested to me that Peter could have argued that none of his answers to the questions in the courtyard were strictly false. Each one is ambiguous: 'I am not' (18:17, 25) doesn't specify what he is not, and the third accusation was that he was *seen* in the garden (18:26), and Peter could have been denying that he was seen, but not that he was there. Peter might have decided to report back to the others that he had managed to use clever answers to avoid strictly lying, whilst staying under cover.

Peter could have told the story of that night so differently, emphasizing how, whereas everyone else ran away, with courage and great cunning he continued to follow Jesus, how he remained under cover, pretending to be an enemy to stay close to Jesus, fooling people and giving indirect answers to avoid lying. But he doesn't. He was so free of his past that he was able to share it, knowing he was forgiven and free. And being free of his past meant he was also free to move into the future that Jesus had for him.

DECONSTRUCTING OUR IDENTITY

Here Jesus calls Peter by his old name, 'Simon son of John' (21:15, 16, 17). The name he was given before his failure, 'Peter', or 'rock' was different, unique even, and was meant to signify that he would stand strong and be faithful to the end. And no one else had this name. He was unique, and confident in his uniqueness. When Jesus predicts that all of them will fall away, Peter feels confident that he is different – that even if everyone runs away, he is willing to die with Jesus. But now Jesus reminds him that he is neither rock solid nor unique.

Jesus strips Peter of his unique name and calls him Simon. Simon was not a unique name. In fact, Simon was the most common name in Palestine at that time. Of the top ninety-nine names given to people living in that place at that time, Simon was the most common.[*] There are eight people in the New Testament called Simon. And John was the fifth most common name at the time. There are at least five people called John in the New Testament. So, in calling him 'Simon son of John', Jesus was reminding him that he was no different to anyone else.

Sometimes you come across people who say that they are 'deconstructing their faith', but here we find Jesus deconstructing Peter. Jesus strips everything away from Peter, including his sense of his own identity, until all that is left is just Simon son of John being asked whether he loves Jesus.

When everything is stripped away, we can be left just with the self, and the result is individualism, isolation, loneliness and the weight of the world on each of our shoulders. Or we find ourselves left with nothing, and the result is despair. But there is one more option, which is that when everything is taken away we are left with this: Jesus sitting across the fire from us and asking us if we love him. And that is the foundation of the purpose of our lives.

FOLLOWING YOUR OWN PATH

After breakfast Peter walks along the beach with Jesus, discussing his future, and then he turns to see 'the other disciple', probably John, and asks, 'What about him?' (21:21). And Jesus responds by telling him, in effect, 'Don't worry about his purpose. Just follow me and do what I'm calling you to do.'

Community is essential for rediscovering our purpose. Earlier in this story, when they realize the miraculous size of their catch, it was this disciple who pointed out to Peter that it was Jesus speaking to them from the shore, his voice calling across the water telling them where to fish (21:7). It is in community that we learn to hear God's voice, and where we give each other the courage to follow his voice.

---

[*] Palestinian Jews living in the period 330 BC – 200 AD, from Richard Bauckham, *Jesus and the Eyewitnesses* (William B Eerdmans Publishing Co, 2006), p70.

But our call is unique. It is easy to get distracted by what is happening to everyone else. We look at other people's lifestyles, their choices, their successes, and lose track of God's unique purpose for us. We can spend our time trying to be the same as everyone else, or we can use all our effort to try to be different from everyone else. Either way we are not following Jesus.

Peter was highly competitive, and particularly with this other disciple. He had raced with him on the way to the empty tomb (20:3–4). Here he races the boat to the shore, swimming while the others row back (21:7–8). Jesus needs to break this competitiveness, and says 'Don't worry about him, your great friend and rival, just love me and follow me.'

This other disciple was also his companion. They did so much together. They were there together when Jairus' daughter was raised from the dead. They were there together at the Transfiguration.* They were together at the empty tomb (20:3–8). Peter may also have been asking, 'Will he be with me? Will we get to do this together?' But Jesus says, 'Don't worry about him. If necessary, you may have to go alone. But you won't be alone because I am with you.'

This was one of the most painful aspects of our call to Brazil. After thirteen years working together with the same group of people, friends with whom we had done everything, Jesus was calling us to go, even if it meant going alone. Part of receiving the call of God on our lives is being willing to go when others don't, or being willing to go where others aren't.

LOVING JESUS

Everything flows from the love of Jesus. Jesus is recommissioning Peter, but the only question he asks is whether Peter loves him. Our purpose emerges from our love for Jesus. We love Jesus and so we do what he asks us to do.

* Mark 5:37; Matthew 17:1.

When Peter goes fishing at the start of this story, it looks like he is simply doing what he wants. He decides, 'I'm going out to fish' (21:3). There is no suggestion that he thinks it would be good to go fishing or that it is right to go fishing. He just wants to do it. But Jesus is going to help him move towards something greater, because of Peter's love for Jesus. Throughout John's Gospel Jesus connects love and obedience (e.g. 14:23). Love is listening to God's voice and doing what he asks us to do.

Our calling is based on our love for Jesus. This is true, even when it feels like this love is so small and fragile. When Jesus first asks Peter if he loves him, he uses the word *agapao* for love and asks him whether he loves him more than the other disciples do. Peter responds very simply that he loves him, not claiming a superior love to the other disciples. He uses a different word, *philo*, for love. When Peter had claimed to be willing to die with Jesus even if everyone else abandoned him, he was claiming to love Jesus more than the others. But now he will not make that claim, and deliberately avoids using the same word for love that Jesus uses. Jesus asks again, 'Do you love me?' (*agapao*) and Peter again avoids using the same word for love. He replies, 'I love you' (*philo*). It is as if he cannot bring himself to claim the same love for Jesus as he has experienced from Jesus for himself. Finally, Jesus adopts the same word that Peter is using, and asks him, 'Do you love me?' (*philei*) and Peter uses that same word in response, 'I love you' (*philo*).*

Peter no longer wants to claim a great love for Jesus, certainly nothing greater than anyone else. But for Jesus that is enough. All he wants is our imperfect, flawed efforts at loving him. He's saying, 'Don't worry about who you are. Just love me and we'll work it out. And don't worry about being unique or being the same as everyone

---

* There is some debate amongst commentators as to the significance of the different words for love, and whether *agapao* and *philo* had different meanings at this time, or whether they are simply used interchangeably. The interesting thing here is Peter's avoidance of the same word that Jesus uses.

else. Just love me. Love me and you will fulfil the great purpose I have for you.'

There is a beautiful culmination to this conversation. Peter knows now that his love is weak and conditional, and he won't claim anything more than this. But then Jesus tells him that in the end Peter will lay down his life for Jesus. Instead of protecting himself he will give himself up. And instead of doing what he wants, his hands will be tied, and he will go where he doesn't want to go (21:18). Instead of denying Jesus he will glorify Jesus (21:19). The one who had messed up so badly is called once again, and this time he will do what he was not able to do before, and he would fulfil the extraordinary calling that Jesus had given him.

It is the same for you and me. No matter what has happened in the past, Jesus is still calling, renewing and restoring us. He is asking us to love him. And through that love our purpose will be fulfilled.

Chapter 19

MEETING JESUS
AND EVERYTHING
CHANGING

Paul

Acts 9

As he neared Damascus on his journey, suddenly a light from heaven flashed around him. He fell to the ground and heard a voice say to him, 'Saul, Saul, why do you persecute me?'

'Who are you, Lord?' Saul asked.

'I am Jesus, whom you are persecuting,' he replied. 'Now get up and go into the city, and you will be told what you must do.'

ACTS 9:3–6

By blood and origin, I am all Albanian. My citizenship is Indian. I am a Catholic nun. As to my calling, I belong to the whole world. As to my heart, I belong entirely to Jesus.

MOTHER TERESA*

Henry Moorhouse was born in Manchester in 1840. He was a gang leader and had depression. He always carried a loaded gun with him, not to use on others, but to use on himself if he was ever consumed with despair. On a cold winter night in 1861 he was

---

* Ruth A. Tucker, *Extraordinary Women of Christian History: What we can Learn from their Struggles and Triumphs* (Baker Books, 2016), p464.

passing the Alhambra Circus in Manchester when he heard voices coming from within. Thinking a fight was taking place, he rushed in ready to join in, but instead found a gathering in which someone was explaining the gospel. As soon as he heard the name 'Jesus' his heart was pierced. He became a preacher, speaking to millions in the US and UK. One of the people on whom he had a profound impact was a preacher called DL Moody, who would become the greatest evangelist of the nineteenth century. Moorhouse became known as 'the man who moved the man who moved the world.'*

When Jesus enters our lives, everything changes. We might be going in the wrong direction. We might have a false sense of who we are supposed to be. We might feel drawn to the wrong people for the wrong reasons. We might spend our whole lives pursuing the wrong things. But then we meet the one who changes everything.

Saul, later known as Paul, had a strong sense of purpose for his life. He had a clear vision. He knew what to do and how to do it. He was highly motivated, passionate and ambitious. He was well-trained and well-educated, and apparently effective in what he was attempting to do. The only problem was that it was the wrong vision. He was trying to do the wrong things, for the wrong reasons, with and for the wrong people. But then Jesus enters his story in a dramatic way, redirecting him, recreating him and reconnecting him. His previous mission is abandoned, and a much greater calling begins. For whenever Jesus enters our lives, everything begins to change.

REDIRECTED

When Jesus enters our lives, he redirects us. As Paul is travelling along the road towards Damascus, with a plan to arrest the followers of Jesus, Jesus himself confronts him, saying to him, 'Saul, Saul, why

---

* Henry Moorhouse, 'Chief men among the Brethren Biography', *Brethren Archive*, brethrenarchive.org (accessed May 2024).

do you persecute me?' (9:4). He is asking him, 'What are you doing? You think you're doing the right things, defending your nation, trying to help your own people, defending the way things have been done before, but you're attacking me.' Jesus confronts Paul, showing him that he is on the wrong path, and that his actions are an attack on the Lord himself.

Whether we realize it or not, our whole lives are about our relationship with Jesus. We might try to make more money because we don't trust that Jesus will provide. We might try to please people because we don't trust that Jesus really approves of us. We seek satisfaction in all kinds of things because we're not sure that Jesus fulfils us completely. At every moment, either we are running away from him or moving towards him, either we are attacking him or embracing him, either persecuting him or proclaiming him, either refusing his love or letting his love in.

Jesus confronts each of us today, just as he confronted Paul. He asks us: Why are you persecuting me? Why are you avoiding me? Why are you ignoring me? Why are you fighting me? Why are you resisting me? Why are you running from me? Why are you holding back from me?

Jesus then sets Paul on a new path, telling him to 'go into the city, and you will be told what you must do' (9:6). Jesus is saying, in effect, 'You're doing the wrong things. Your current plans are not right. You don't know what you should be doing. You don't have the right instincts for what is right. But you will find out. I will show you.'

Jesus tells Paul to take the first step: 'Go into the city'. Take the first step and then the rest will become clear. This verse was a great help to us when we first felt called to go to Rio. We sensed that God was calling us to Brazil, and to Rio de Janeiro, and to Christ Church in particular, but were not clear on what we were supposed to do once we got here. People would ask us what our vision was, and our answer was, 'Our vision is to get there.' But we trusted that God would show us what to do when we got there.

Often God just gives us the first step. We want to know the whole story, but God simply tells us what to do next: 'Go to the city'. Later God will direct him to preach the gospel, to plant churches, to appoint elders and to write letters. But the first step was simply to go to the place where God is asking him to go.

Notice the 'must'. For there to be a calling there needs to be a 'must'. In Western culture there has long been an emphasis on the pursuit of freedom. Freedom is a beautiful thing and ultimately comes from God. The foundational story for the people of God in the Old Testament was liberation from slavery in Egypt. A central theme in the saving work of Jesus is the promise of freedom, for 'if the Son sets you free you will be free indeed.'* But if freedom becomes detached from all other virtues, like justice, love or goodness, it begins to make life feel meaningless. Societies which idolize freedom also have crises of purpose, for freedom becomes the attempt to remove all obligations. But if there are no 'musts', there is no purpose. Jesus was calling Paul to something that included a 'must'.

And here we have a paradox, for in discovering his purpose, Paul would find a freedom he had never known before. He would describe himself as God's servant, or a 'slave' of Jesus Christ, but also write about the wonderful freedom of knowing Jesus.** Jesus is the only one who can answer our longing for freedom and purpose. When we give our lives to him, we discover both perfect freedom and a perfect purpose.

This new direction for Paul will not be easy. Jesus appears to an existing disciple, Ananias, letting him know that he will show Paul, 'how much he must suffer for my name' (9:16). One of the first things that Paul is going to have to learn is that he is going to suffer. This doesn't seem like the best form of advertising for Christianity. I can imagine Ananias' friends talking to him about going to see Paul, saying to him, 'This is a big moment, don't mess

* John 8:36.
** Romans 1:1; Galatians 5:1.

it up. This could change everything for us. Remember to tell him all about the unconditional love, the deep peace, stories of healing, total forgiveness, the removal of shame, the transformation we've all experienced, the hope of eternal life and the unspeakable joy of knowing Jesus.' And Ananias replying, 'I'm actually going to go and tell him how much he has to suffer!'

And he will suffer. After becoming a Christian, Paul will be beaten, shipwrecked, imprisoned and eventually executed for his faith. As Dietrich Bonhoeffer famously put it, 'When Christ calls a man, he bids him come and die.'* He's not choosing the easy option, but he does so because he knows it is true. He knows it is right. He's met Jesus. And so, whatever difficulty he is going to experience is worth it all.

His encounter takes place at noon (22:6), when the sun was at its highest, but now he has met one who was brighter than the noonday sun. He has heard a voice greater than any other voice. He's seen something better than all the suffering that the world could throw at him. He had been there when Stephen was stoned for preaching the gospel and saw his face shine like that of an angel (6:15) even when he was surrounded by hatred and violence. And he had met on the road to Damascus someone with the power greater than death, who had never stopped loving him, despite everything he had done. In Jesus he had met one who was worth everything.

Our instinct is often to seek comfort and safety, staying in control and choosing the easy option. But Jesus redirects us, because what he has for us is something far more difficult, more painful, but infinitely more significant, fulfilling and delightful than what we would choose for ourselves.

RECREATED

This encounter with Jesus also recreates Paul. Paul is doing the wrong things and he's doing them for the wrong reasons. The passage starts by

* Dietrich Bonhoeffer, *The Cost of Discipleship* (SCM, 2001), p44.

saying that Paul 'was still breathing out murderous threats against the Lord's disciples' (9:1). He's breathing out hatred and anger, emanating from the core of who he is. His whole being is filled with hatred.

What are we breathing out? Is it fear, or hatred, or selfish ambition? At the end of John's Gospel, Jesus breathes on the disciples, giving them the Holy Spirit, and the fruit of the Spirit is love, joy, peace, patience, goodness, kindness, gentleness, faithfulness and self-control.* Either we are breathing out the fruit of the Spirit, or we will breathe out something very different.

Jesus calls out to Paul and says to him, 'Saul, Saul' (9:4). When God calls us, it is by name. And there is often a repetition of the name of the person God is calling. He says, 'Abraham, Abraham', 'Jacob, Jacob', 'Moses, Moses', and 'Samuel, Samuel.' When he comforts Martha and when he warns Peter,** he uses this repetition of their names. It is a way of saying, 'I know you.' The twentieth-century American writer and speaker, Dale Carnegie, wrote, 'A person's name is to that person the sweetest and most important sound in any language.'*** Jesus calls him by name. He says, 'I know you.' And he speaks to him in Aramaic, his native language, the language of his heart. He is reassuring him that he knows him completely, how he feels, what he thinks and what he wants.

And then Jesus recreates Saul. He knows him, and now he needs to remake him. There is a great light. It's noon in Israel. Noon in England might not be quite so significant, but noon in Israel, or Brazil, means a strong sun. But there is a light that is even stronger. When God made the world, the first thing he made was 'light'. Now there is another light, and another creation. In addition, there is a voice from heaven. When God made the world, he created through his voice. Now God is using his voice for a new creation. Paul is thrown to the ground.

* John 20:22; Galatians 5:22–23.
** Genesis 22:11; 46:2; Exodus 3:4; 1 Samuel 3:10; Luke 10:41; 22:31.
*** Dale Carnegie, *How to Win Friends and Influence People* (Simon & Schuster, 2009), p117.

When God made the first human being, Adam, it was from the dust in the ground; now Paul is going to be reformed from the ground. Later, Paul will write that anyone who is in Christ is 'a new creation.'*

Jesus recreates him by humbling him. Paul was a highly impressive person. His Jewish credentials were impeccable.** He had studied under the greatest rabbis of the day. He was intelligent, influential and honoured by other Jews from a young age (7:58). He was a rising star in the greatest religious system in the world. He was also educated in Greek culture and philosophy, a brilliant speaker and writer. And he was a citizen of Rome, the greatest empire the world had ever known (22:3–5, 25–28). But all of this is now stripped away. Jesus wants to start again with him.

So now he is blind and has to be led by the hand. The one who was so clever, knowledgeable and perceptive cannot see anything. Paul, the great scholar, is unable to read. The great leader is told what to do. The rising star is led by the hand by others, as if he were a child. And then Jesus sends to him not Peter, or one of the twelve apostles, but a simple disciple called Ananias who doesn't get mentioned in the book of Acts again.

Jesus appears to be saying to him that all those things which he thought were important before really do not matter. He needs to be stripped of his pride. Later Paul will write that all his Jewish credentials he now considers rubbish. To the Greek world he would claim that he had neither wise nor persuasive words. To the Roman world he would write as one who was a slave, and if he was a citizen of anywhere, he was a citizen of heaven.***

Everything which he might previously have thought impressive or important: his education or achievements, his connections or the opinions of others, have been removed. And his identity is renewed and made much stronger. From now on his identity would be found

---

* Genesis 1:3; 2:7; 2 Corinthians 5:17.
** Philippians 3:4–6.
*** Philippians 3:8; 1 Corinthians 2:4; Philippians 3:20.

'in Christ' and he would be one who is loved by God.

When I first met Tara and we started dating, I was keen to impress her. And so I invited her to the church where I was preaching, but she refused because she was part of a different church. Then I got her to come along and watch me play rugby on a Saturday afternoon. This time she accepted, and, knowing that she was there, I played better than I had ever done before, scoring lots of tries, often right in front of where she was sitting. I asked her after the game what she thought of the match, and she said she hadn't seen any of it because she was chatting to the person next to her. I quickly realized that none of my attempts to impress her worked, and yet I discovered that she still loved me.

This is what Paul was discovering. He needed to be stripped of everything just to know that he was loved for who he was. He becomes like a newborn child who cannot do anything for himself, has not achieved anything, has nothing to offer the world, who cannot feed or care for or protect himself, and yet is perfectly loved.

RECONNECTED

Jesus comes into Paul's life, redirecting him and recreating him. And then he reconnects him. For Paul has been doing the wrong things, for the wrong reasons, and he's been doing them with and for the wrong people. His authority has come from the high priest, and he's seeking out the Jewish Christians to put an end to their activities, trying to shut down this new movement before it gets any momentum. He's being influenced by the wrong people, trying to impress the wrong people, working alongside the wrong people, to have an impact on the wrong people.

Now Jesus connects him with some new people. Ananias comes into his life. He calls him 'brother' even though they have never met, and Paul has caused so much fear and trauma for the first Christians (9:17). Ananias lays his hands on him and prays for him (9:17). As a result, Paul receives back his sight and is strengthened (9:18–19). These new friends seem to love him unconditionally, praying for him and literally helping him to see in new ways. They give him strength, whereas his old 'friends' will immediately try to destroy him when they discover that he has become a follower of Jesus (9:23–24). It's important that we have people in our lives who love us, pray for us and give us strength.

This story of Paul's conversion occurs three times in Acts. In each account, it mentions his travelling companions, but there are slight differences in the details. In the first account, they hear something but do not see Jesus (9:7). In the second, they see the light, but don't understand the voice (22:9). In the third, Paul says that he alone heard the voice, unlike his companions (26:14). So, his companions hear something but don't understand. They see something but cannot see Jesus.

Paul spends much of the rest of his life travelling around the world, telling people the good news about Jesus, and he always takes travelling companions – Barnabas and John Mark, Silas and Luke – but these are travelling companions who know Jesus, who recognize him and who listen to his voice. In the great journey of life which is so tough and challenging, full of difficulties and temptations, we too need to have travelling companions, who know Jesus and hear his voice.

Paul is going to be sent to a whole new group of people. His previous world was predominantly Jewish. He spent time with Jews, lived with Jews, worshipped with Jews and persecuted Jews whom he thought were getting it wrong. But now God was calling him to the Gentiles, to the non-Jews. This didn't make much sense. He was the most Jewish of Jews, but called to those who were unlike him.

When Tara first mentioned Brazil to me about sixteen years ago, I dismissed it quickly, for I like speaking, reading and listening in English. I'm not very good at new, unfamiliar places, and especially not foreign languages. The temptation is always to stay with people who are like us. And it doesn't make much sense for God to send an

English family to minister in Brazil. Surely a Brazilian family would be more effective in reaching Brazilians. But God often calls us to people who are unlike us. And here God calls the Jewish Paul to extend his work among the Gentiles.

And he will get his authority from a new source. Before his authority came from the high priest, but now he has another authority. When he first meets Jesus, he calls him, 'Lord'. This word can simply be used as a title of respect, like 'Sir', or it can be used to refer to 'The Lord', as in God himself, the one who directs our lives, the one who has all authority. Here it is unclear how Paul is using this word, but soon there will be no doubt, for Paul will repeatedly write of Jesus as his Lord, his master, the one who will direct his life and from whom all authority derives.

We know from Paul's letter to the Galatians, that after this encounter Paul goes into Arabia. This is an interesting choice. He doesn't go to Jerusalem, the centre of Judaism. He doesn't go to Athens or Alexandria, the cultural centres of Greek philosophy. He doesn't go to Rome, the political heart of the Roman Empire. He goes to Arabia, to the desert. Why? Perhaps he needed to hear God's voice for himself. He needed to process what had just happened. He needed to know what Jesus was saying just to him. In Paul's writings he only mentions Arabia twice. Once to refer to where he went after his conversion, and the other is when he mentions the location of Mount Sinai in Arabia.* Mount Sinai was the place where God spoke to Moses. Perhaps he went to the place to hear the voice of God. He needed to hear from God himself, away from all the noise. He needed to hear from the one who, from now on, would be the director of his life.

When Jesus appears on the road to Damascus, Paul asks this question: 'Who are you, Lord?' (9:5). This is the most important question we can ever ask. This is the crucial question which reveals our calling.

* Galatians 1:17; 4:25.

We can sometimes think that the most important question is 'Lord, who am I?' but Paul doesn't receive his calling by discovering his own identity, rather he discovers the identity of Jesus. For his calling was not going to be based on his character, but on the character of Jesus; not on his own purposes, but the purposes of God. Our greatest problem is not an insufficient view of ourselves, but an insufficient view of Jesus. He is the perfect one, the beautiful one, the humble servant and the everlasting God, the healer, the great teacher and the lover of our souls. He is the crucified one and the resurrected one. He is the one with the great and perfect purpose, and the one from whom all purpose derives. And he calls us to himself, to love him and to join in with his great purpose.

PART FIVE

Keep Going

Chapter 20

GOING AGAIN

The Great Commission
Matthew 28

---

*Then the eleven disciples went to Galilee, to the mountain where
Jesus had told them to go. When they saw him, they worshipped
him; but some doubted. Then Jesus came to them and said, 'All
authority in heaven and on earth has been given to me. Therefore
go and make disciples of all nations, baptizing them in the name
of the Father and of the Son and of the Holy Spirit, and teaching
them to obey everything I have commanded you. And surely I am
with you always, to the very end of the age.'*

MATTHEW 28:16–20

Roads? Where we're going, we don't need roads.

BACK TO THE FUTURE*

Becoming a Christian means becoming part of a community with a
purpose. At the end of Matthew's Gospel, Jesus sends out his eleven
disciples, giving them the purpose which has become the purpose
of the Church: to go, make disciples of all nations, baptizing and
teaching everyone to obey everything that he has commanded.

It is an *expansive* purpose, for it is to 'all nations' (Matthew 28:19).
It requires us to 'go', to move and be courageous. Our lives can easily
shrink over time. A love for all people can become a love for people

---

* Robert Zemeckis, *Back to the Future* (Universal Pictures, 1985).

like us. A heart for the nations can become a love for only our nation. Instead of serving the community, we serve ourselves. We go from loving our neighbour as ourselves, to just loving ourselves. Martin Luther defined sin as *homo incurvatus in se*, literally 'humanity curved in on itself', and our natural tendency is to become curved in on ourselves. We naturally shrink and the vision for our lives can shrink. But Jesus gives us an expansive purpose, one that forces us to look outwards.

It is an *impossible* purpose. Jesus gives us a mission which is far too big for us to do. He commanded his eleven disciples to go and 'make disciples of all nations.' The global population at the time of the Great Commission was around 170–400 million people. Even if we took the lowest estimate, that's roughly 15.5 million people for each of these eleven disciples to convert, baptize and teach. It's impossible and requires the miraculous. For God's purposes require God's power. Our mission will need miracles.

INTIMACY AND DIFFICULTY

God's purpose for our lives is expansive and impossible. And, as we've seen so often through these stories, it starts with intimacy with Jesus. We read that 'Jesus came to them' (28:18). The purpose of their lives emerges from their relationship with Jesus. If we want to have more purpose in our lives, we need to spend time with Jesus. For he is the one with the great purpose, and all purpose flows from him.

It also emerges out of pain and difficulty. The first words of this section, 'the *eleven* disciples' (28:16) remind us that already something has gone wrong. There were supposed to be twelve of them, but Judas had betrayed Jesus and then killed himself. So they would still have been processing the actions and death of one of their closest friends and companions, someone with whom they had shared everything over these past three years.

Over the previous days, events had not turned out as they thought they would. They had seen their leader, the one they had left everything to follow, humiliated and tortured, dying on a cross. Their movement had seemingly ended in failure, and everything had fallen apart. And, in this time of crisis, all of them (except possibly John) had messed up in some way, either abandoning or denying Jesus. So mixed in with the pain and grief are shame and regret and an awareness of their own weaknesses. But there is also joy and wonder, for Jesus had been raised to life, death had been defeated and they had been reconciled with the one they loved. And they respond with worship. When they see Jesus, they worship him (28:17). They are in pain, but they worship Jesus. They have messed up, but they worship Jesus.

But there's also doubt and confusion (28:17). Even after everything they've seen, the miracles, the teaching, the perfect character of Jesus Christ, there are still so many questions. They have seen him raised from the dead. This has filled them with joy, but it was also confusing. It didn't fit with how they thought history would work. So they are excited, worshipping him, but also full of doubt, not sure how to behave as a result.

There is a mixture of joy and pain, intimacy and doubt, faith and confusion. And out of all of this, their purpose emerges.

OBEDIENCE AND RESISTANCE

There is also a combination of obedience and resistance. They are trying to do what Jesus asked them to do, going to the mountain 'where Jesus had told them to go' (28:16). They are being obedient, despite the doubts, despite the disappointments. It's a reminder that, in the toughest and most confusing times, we need to keep on doing the things which Jesus has asked us to do and, in the joy-filled and exciting times, we need to keep on following the instructions which Jesus has given us.

Travelling to the mountain where Jesus had told them to go was a relatively small act of obedience, compared with what Jesus was going to ask them to do for the rest of their lives. Before being told to go to the nations they were told to go to this mountain. The big moves tend to follow small moves. We learn obedience in the small things so that we can also be obedient in the big things. If we are searching for our life's purpose, it is best to start with the small acts of obedience to the commands of Jesus – as we follow him in the smaller matters, he calls us to the bigger adventures.

But there is also resistance ahead for these disciples, for God's call on our lives is never easy. It wasn't easy for these disciples to go. Here Jesus gives them a command, which is clear and undeniable: go and make disciples of all nations. Soon after this, God sends his Spirit at Pentecost, giving them the gift of speaking in tongues, which gave them the ability to communicate with all the people of different nationalities who were gathered in Jerusalem, so that each of them heard the gospel in their own language. They had been told to go to all nations, and then given the ability to go to all those nations.

And yet thirty years after Jesus had given this command and equipped them with the Spirit at Pentecost, it looks like all these disciples who were still alive are still in Jerusalem, and that they had outsourced the going to the nations to Paul and Silas, Barnabas and Luke, and John Mark and Apollos, to those later Christians who had not been there on this hillside. Maybe, as we are often tempted to do, they had persuaded other people to do what they themselves had been commanded to do.

It's always difficult to obey the voice of Jesus. The instinct to stay where we are is strong. But God calls us to go. Sometimes it takes something dramatic to get us moving. For the disciples it is believed to have been the fall of Jerusalem, when the city was destroyed by the Romans in AD 70. For, though it took thirty years to get them moving, within a few years Thomas was heading to Syria, Philip to Carthage in North Africa, Andrew to Russia, Turkey and Greece,

Matthew to Persia and then Ethiopia, Bartholomew to India, Armenia and Saudi Arabia, James to Syria (where he was clubbed to death), Simon the Zealot to Persia (where he was sawn in two), and John to Ephesus in Turkey. Despite their initial resistance, they would be obedient to the command of Jesus in the end.

THE PROMISE OF THE PRESENCE

So there is worship and there is doubt; there is intimacy and uncertainty; there is obedience and resistance. They have had the lows of Good Friday and the highs of Easter Sunday. They have gone through confusion and heartbreak. And from all of this, Jesus calls them to their great purpose. Through all the complications and emotions of life, Jesus calls us and gives us purpose.

And it is not about us. Jesus starts his words of commission by saying that all authority had been given to him (28:18). The foundation of the disciples' calling and purpose, and the foundation of our calling and purpose, is the authority of Jesus to command us, and he can do all things.

Jesus does not look at his disciples and say, 'You guys are amazing. You're compassionate, brave, wise and courageous. You can do anything you put your minds to. So now go, use all your gifts and talents, and fulfil your wonderful potential.' Their purpose is not based on them, but on Jesus. And in the same way, our purpose is not based on us, but on Jesus. It emerges from him, is made possible by him and it is all for him.

And this great call on our lives ends with a promise: 'And surely I am with you always, to the very end of the age' (28:20). Jesus says, 'surely' – it is a promise. Never doubt this. Matthew's Gospel began with the promise of the coming of 'Immanuel', which means 'God with us'* and it ends with the promise of Jesus remaining with us forever. This is the promise which makes everything possible.

* Matthew 1:23.

He is with us forever. Life is always changing, but Jesus promises to be with us always. Everything else can and will change; he alone is constant. And he is with us wherever we go. He promises to be with us just as much in Rio de Janeiro as in Brighton.

And it is, 'I will be with you' not 'You will always be together.' For God's purposes to be fulfilled they had to leave one another and go to the nations. If they had stayed together, we wouldn't be here today. Sometimes we are called to head off in different directions. In Tolkien's *The Lord of the Rings* a 'Fellowship of the Ring' is formed to achieve the great quest of destroying the ring of power. This Fellowship wins many great battles and succeeds in making progress towards their goal. But they reach a point when the Fellowship must split up in order for them to fulfil their purposes. Aragorn, Legolas and Gimli need to go to Rohan. Frodo and Sam have to go to Mordor. Gandalf must fight the Balrog. Merry and Pippin need to summon the Ents to war.

Everything changes, but Jesus promises to be with us always. It is not the promise that everything will be OK. He does not guarantee success in everything we attempt. But he promises to be with us. This is the only promise we need. For God's presence enables us to fulfil our purpose. But God's presence also *is* our purpose. We were made for him, and our hearts long for him. Before anything else we are called to Jesus, to love him and be loved by him. This is our great purpose: to know God's love and enjoy him forever.